ACIM GUIDE TO A MIRACULOUS LIFE

Manifesting with *A Course in Miracles*

Elizabeth M. Herrera

Published by Blue Gator Inc.

First printing, July 2024

ACIM Guide to a Miraculous Life was written for students of *A Course in Miracles* (ACIM) who wish to explore the Course's teachings on transforming their lives within the Dream (illusion) to achieve happiness, well-being and abundance in a way that is harmonious with their spirit and God's Will.

Many of the quotes in the book are from *A Course in Miracles*, copyright ©1992, 1999, 2007 by the Foundation for Inner Peace, acim.org.

Portions of the names, locations, and other identifying information in the true-life portions have been changed to protect the people's privacy. When first mentioned, fictional names are indicated with quotation marks.

Contents

Introduction ... 1

Preface ... 12

Overview of the Miraculous Life Process ... 32

Time Can Work for You ... 45

You Can Use Emotions as a Barometer ... 53

Release the Blockages to Abundance ... 60

Exercise — Releasing the Blockages ... 70

Envision the Future as If It is Happening Now ... 77

How to Move Forward ... 86

Exercise — Discovering What You Want ... 99

Watch Out for the Speed Bumps ... 106

You Are Powerful Beyond Measure ... 125

Exercise — The Secret to Miraculous Results ... 133

Connecting with God ... 140

Exercise — Connecting with God ... 142

Exercise — Bringing in the Divine Power ... 144

Summary of the Miraculous Life Process ... 146

Journal — 60-Days of Reflection ... 153

Explanation of the ACIM Annotation System ... 184

Overview of Shamanism and Shamanic Journeying ... 186

About the Author ... 189

Acknowledgments

I extend my heartfelt gratitude to David Beaver, Eric Hunt, Sharon Monroe and Niki Orietas for their contributions to this book.

This book is dedicated to the spiritual seekers, mystics, miracle workers, teachers and students whose search for the light brightens the world.

"This is not a course in the play of ideas, but in their practical application. Nothing could be more specific than to be told that if you ask you will receive."

T-11.VIII.5.3-4

Introduction

"Change but your mind on what you want to see, and all the world must change accordingly." W-pI.132.5.2

ACIM Guide to a Miraculous Life was written for students of *A Course in Miracles* (ACIM) who wish to explore the Course's teachings on transforming their lives within the Dream (illusion) to achieve happiness, well-being and abundance in a way that is harmonious with their spirit and God's Will.

"Your Father knoweth that you have need of nothing. In Heaven this is so, for what could you need in eternity? In your world you do need things. It is a world of scarcity in which you find yourself *because* you are lacking. Yet can you find yourself in such a world? Without the Holy Spirit the answer would be no. Yet because of Him the answer is a joyous *yes!* As Mediator between the two worlds, He knows what

you have need of and what will not hurt you."
T-13.VII.10.2-9

The Course asserts that our higher Mind, which is still asleep in heaven, created this world as an illusionary dream. Unfortunately, the Dream was so realistic that we became imprisoned in it, but God did not abandon us without hope. He called on the Holy Spirit to help us escape from the Dream so we can return home.

"When you have been caught in the world of perception you are caught in a dream. You cannot escape without help, because everything your senses show merely witnesses to the reality of the dream. God has provided the Answer, the only Way out, the true Helper. It is the function of His Voice, His Holy Spirit, to mediate between the two worlds. He can do this because, while on the one hand He knows the truth, on the other He also recognizes our illusions, but without believing in them. It is the Holy Spirit's goal to help us escape from the dream world by teaching us how to reverse our thinking and unlearn our mistakes." ACIM Preface

We will wake up, regardless of whether we work with the Holy Spirit or simply let the Dream play out as it was originally dreamed. But if we don't heal the unloving aspects of the Dream, it will take millions of years for it to reach its original ending, and that is a lot of needless suffering.

"Just as the separation occurred over millions of years, the Last Judgment will extend over a similarly long period, and perhaps an even longer one. Its length can, however, be greatly shortened by miracles, the device for shortening but not abolishing time." T-2.VIII.2.5-6

Our worldly accomplishments and the illusion of separation will fade away upon our awakening. But until that moment arrives, with each healed aspect of the Dream — where pain, suffering, poverty and fear vanish — we not only benefit ourselves, but also uplift all of humanity, hastening our collective awakening.

The Holy Spirit uses our everyday experiences to teach us how to awaken from the Dream sooner. But we still have to manage our daily responsibilities, such as paying our bills, filling our days and interacting with others, so we might as well do all these things in a way that brings us joy and allows us to recognize and express our true nature of love.

"You will not remember change and shift in Heaven. You have need of contrast only here. Contrast and differences are necessary teaching aids, for by them you learn what to avoid and what to seek." T-13.XI.6.1-3

"The ego made the world as it perceives it, but the Holy Spirit, the reinterpreter of what the ego made, sees the world as a teaching device for bringing you home." T-5.III.11:1

Through the Miraculous Life Process, you will co-create with the Holy Spirit, Jesus and divine helpers to unlock the boundless potential within yourself and manifest an amazing life.

> "We only start again an ancient journey long ago begun that but seems new. We have begun again upon a road we travelled on before and lost our way a little while. And now we try again. Our new beginning has the certainty the journey lacked till now. Look up and see His Word among the stars, where He has set your Name along with His. Look up and find your certain destiny the world would hide but God would have you see." C-ep.3.2-7

Let go of the belief that sacrificing or embracing poverty signifies spiritual superiority. In the Bible, Jesus multiplied two small fish and five loaves of bread to feed a large group of hungry people, and turned water into wine at a wedding. He even instructed his disciple Peter to find a gold coin in a fish's mouth to pay taxes. Jesus effortlessly met his needs through miracles. In *A Course in Miracles*, Jesus explained that his crucifixion "...was the Sonship's last useless journey, and it represents release from fear to anyone who understands it." There is no need for further sacrifice.

Core Concepts of the Miraculous Life Process:

- The mind is an incredible source of power that is constantly creating. There are no idle thoughts — every single one has the potential to alter your life. By harnessing the power of your mind and trusting in your abilities, you can achieve incredible things beyond your wildest dreams.

  "The mind is very powerful, and never loses its creative force. It never sleeps. Every instant it is creating. It is hard to recognize that thought and belief combine into a power surge that can literally move mountains. It appears at first glance that to believe such power about yourself is arrogant, but that is not the real reason you do not believe it. You prefer to believe that your thoughts cannot exert real influence because you are actually afraid of them. This may allay awareness of the guilt, but at the cost of perceiving the mind as impotent. If you believe that what you think is ineffectual you may cease to be afraid of it, but you are hardly likely to respect it. There *are* no idle thoughts. All thinking produces form at some level." T-2.VI.9:5-14

- All thoughts contain power, but when combined with strong emotions and beliefs, they become extremely powerful. In this book, you will learn how to maximize the effectiveness of your thoughts.

- It's essential to guard your thoughts with utmost care because they hold the key to manifesting the life you desire.

"If I [Jesus] intervened between your thoughts and their results, I would be tampering with a basic law of cause and effect; the most fundamental law there is. I would hardly help you if I depreciated the power of your own thinking. This would be in direct opposition to the purpose of this course. It is much more helpful to remind you that you do not guard your thoughts carefully enough." T-2.VII.1:4-7

- Because you have Free Will, you can choose whether to focus on loving or unloving thoughts. When your thoughts align with love, you manifest in harmony with your higher self and for the greater good of humanity. When you allow your ego to rule your mind, you form unloving thoughts, such as fear, resentment and guilt that attract undesirable experiences.

"Both miracles and fear come from thoughts. If you are not free to choose one, you would also not be free to choose the other. By choosing the miracle you *have* rejected fear, if only temporarily." T-2.VII.3:1-3

"Fear and love make or create, depending on whether the ego or the Holy Spirit begets or inspires them, but they *will* return to the mind of the thinker and they will affect his total perception." T-7.VI.1.5

- Forgiveness and healing are necessary to remove the blockages that stand between you and the Creative powers, allowing abundance to flow freely into all aspects of your life.

- The Holy Spirit wants you to come to Him for guidance on all matters in your life. With His understanding of all timelines, He is able to offer you more rewarding experiences than you could have ever dreamed of on your own.

  "Only the Holy Spirit knows what you need. For He will give you all things that do not block the way to light. And what else could you need? In time, He gives you all the things that you need have, and will renew them as long as you have need of them. He will take nothing from you as long as you have any need of it." T-13.VII.12.1-5

- Miracles are your divine right. When you co-create with the Holy Spirit, Jesus and divine helpers, you become a miracle worker, creating a more fulfilling life.

- Manifesting your life is not only possible, but something you're already doing whether you realize it or not. You don't need special intuitive abilities. This book will teach you how to *intentionally* manifest with the Divine's help to experience a miraculous life.

Big or Small, Ask for Guidance

How important is it to ask the Holy Spirit, Jesus or divine helpers to assist you with both mundane needs and higher pursuits? According to Jesus himself, both are very important. This example comes from Helen

Schucman's[1] omitted notes about "Guidance" in the URtext[2] of *A Course in Miracles.* In it, Jesus spoke to Schucman about one of her personal decisions.

> "The reason I direct everything that is unimportant is because it is no way to waste your free will. If you insist on doing the trivial your way, you waste too much time and will on it. Will cannot be free if it is tied up in trivia. It never gets out. I will tell you exactly what to do in connection with everything that doesn't matter. That is not an area where choice should be invested. There is better use of time. You have to remember to ask me to take charge of all minutiae, and it will be taken care of so well and so quickly that you cannot bog down in it. The only remaining problem is that you will be unwilling to ask because you are afraid not to be bogged down. Don't let this hold us back. If you will ask, I will arrange these things even if you're not too enthusiastic. Prayer can safely be very specific in little matters. If you need a coat, ask me where to find one. I know your taste well, and I also know where the coat is that you would eventually buy anyway. If you don't like the coat afterwards, that is what would have happened anyway. I did not pick out the coat for you. You said

---

[1] Helen Schucman heard an inner dictation that she scribed in shorthand. William Thetford assisted her by typing out her notes. Their combined efforts resulted in the writing of *A Course in Miracles.*

[2] The URtext is the raw, unedited version of *A Course in Miracles* and contains material the authors felt was too controversial or personal to leave in the final version.

you wanted something warm, inexpensive, and capable of taking rough wear. I told you you could get a Borgana, but I let you get a better one because the furrier needed you. Note, however, that it is better in terms of the criteria you established. I could do this because you saw the coat more that way than in terms of a particular material. You thought of Klein's yourself a few days ago, and then you decided against it, because Borgana is price-fixed. Then you remembered a coat Grace once got there that was much cheaper, and seemed pretty much the same, and asked yourself whether it was really right to be sold on a particular trade name through advertising. That opened your mind. I cannot save you more time than you will let Me, but if you are willing to try the Higher Shopping Service, which also covers all lower-order necessities and even quite a number of whims within reason, I have very good use for the time we could save." URtext, N 4:73-75

In the URtext verse, Jesus expressed to Schucman that he valued her seeking his advice on small matters as a way to save precious time so she could focus on the more important things in life. If he was willing to assist her in finding a coat, I am confident that he is willing to help us with anything we have on our minds.

"There is no situation to which miracles do not apply, and by applying them to all situations you will gain the real world. For in this holy perception you will be made whole, and the Atonement will radiate from your acceptance of it for yourself to everyone the Holy Spirit sends you for your blessing." T-12.VII.1.4-5

In the past, I started the manifestation process many times, but always stopped myself because I feared the process was promoting duality or distracting me from my spiritual path. Now, after applying the Miraculous Life Process and experiencing its results, I believe my former fears were the work of my ego, trying to keep me from working more fully with the Holy Spirit, Jesus and other divine helpers. I had mistakenly thought my practical concerns and worldly desires wouldn't matter to them, but in the URtext verse, Jesus said He very much wants to be a part of everything we do to prevent us from wasting time so we can focus on the more important things in our lives.

You and I can rely on divine guidance for all of our decisions as we move forward with manifesting the life of our dreams.

In This Book, You Will Learn:

- How to manifest an abundant, vibrant and joyful life by co-creating with the Holy Spirit, Jesus and divine helpers.

- How to work with your higher self to discover the great things it has in store for you.

- How to release the blockages between you and the Creative powers so you can fully receive the abundance available to you.

- The secret of connecting with your divine helper to amplify and accelerate your heartfelt desires to a miraculous level.

- Exercises to help you practice each step of the Miraculous Life Process.

- How to avoid the speed bumps that can hinder your manifestation requests.

- You had the power all along!

Preface

Before delving into this book's teachings and transformative exercises, I would like to introduce myself and provide you with a glimpse into my background and experiences.

I was raised in a Christian family in Lansing, Michigan, but lost my faith in my early twenties. My mother aspired to be a missionary, but her plans changed in high school when she fell in love with my handsome Hispanic father. After they married, he attended Spring Arbor University, enrolling in the theology program with the intention of becoming a minister.

The first half of my childhood was idyllic. Our urban neighborhood was a melting pot of kids. One of my fondest memories is of lying on the grass with the other kids as we pointed out the shapes we saw in the white, fluffy clouds. The memories from this time sustained me during the darker periods of growing up.

Our plentiful life abruptly ended when the 1970s recession hit hard, and mortgage interest rates spiked to 17 percent almost overnight, driving my father's house construction business into bankruptcy. To prevent the bank from seizing my father's first, newly constructed house, we moved into it on an acre carved out of his parents' farm in the small rural community of Mason, Michigan.

This poverty-stricken period lasted four years. During this time, my family had very little food and sometimes no heat — a true hardship in Michigan's brutal winters.

My mother had recently completed her teaching degree, but seasoned teachers were being laid off, so a graduate with zero experience stood little chance of being hired. We relied on food stamps, and although we were grateful for the state's assistance, we were also embarrassed. Both of my parents had grown up on farms and were used to being self-reliant. The school lunches were my only full meal. Subsidized by the government, the lunches only cost six cents each, though sometimes my parents didn't even have that. Fortunately, the school let me and my younger siblings run a tab.

Much later, after I had grown up, my mother confessed she had never told us we were poor because she felt we would always be poor as soon as she said it. Somehow, my mother understood the basics of the universal laws of cause and effect, even if it was subconsciously.

While I was in 6th grade, my mother took a job at a local factory, but could only work when they were short-handed. Then she got lucky and received a temporary, six-month secretarial position at the State of Michigan Department of Regulations, which turned into a full-time job. Meanwhile, my father started working at his brother's insulation company. Suddenly, we had health and dental insurance, food and heat!

My parents' combined incomes would have significantly improved our lives, but my father began a string of extra-marital affairs and left. Oddly enough, the household became a more pleasant place to live without the arguing and tension. A year later, my father returned and sat brooding in his chair when he wasn't working. Shortly thereafter, he started his own insulation company, which eventually evolved into a thriving asphalt paving business.

Despite our financial upward momentum, my father was still not mentally committed to our family and continued cheating on my mother. Feeling unloved and unwanted, I became a rebellious teenager who got kicked out of school for smoking cigarettes, skipping school and fighting. My parents stopped talking to me for nearly a year because they were upset with me. They didn't realize (or didn't want to admit) that our family dynamics were contributing to my behavior.

In 9th grade, our class took an assessment test that I didn't realize was the PSAT. I'm sure the teacher told us, but I frequently smoked marijuana in the mornings and was too high to comprehend what was happening. However, I did know the test wouldn't count as a grade, so I rushed through the answers without double-checking. I believed I performed poorly because there were questions I didn't know the answers to.

Several months later, the school's intercom interrupted the classroom and a familiar voice requested that I come down to the office. As I walked through the empty hallways, I assumed I was in trouble again.

Upon my arrival, I was surprised to be escorted into the school counselor's office where he commended me for performing exceptionally well on the PSAT. For several subjects, I tested at the college level.

The counselor asked me why I was flunking several of my classes. I hesitated to tell him about my dysfunctional home and my habit of smoking weed to deal with the pain. So instead, I just shrugged. But then, the counselor told me something that changed my life. He said I could be anything I wanted to be, even a doctor or lawyer, if I put my mind to it.

I contemplated his encouraging words.

Because of my family's chaos and my marijuana use, I had forgotten I used to love school and reading. By focusing on the negative aspects, I had created a vicious cycle in my life. The counselor's words made me realize I had the power within me to overcome my unfortunate circumstances.

To add to my troubles in middle school, I was bullied by a group of girls. When I sought advice from my father, he said I must have done something to deserve it. That shut down the conversation. But despite his callous remark, he was close to the truth. I had allowed my negative thoughts and emotions to control me, attracting people with similar energy. My thoughts were creating my undesirable world. As the Course says, "Thoughts can represent the lower or bodily level of experiences, or the higher or spiritual level of experience." I had chosen poorly.

One night, while my family was driving home, I looked up at the moon and wondered if I would survive this dark period. Then I heard a divine voice whisper, "Only four more years. You can make it." At that moment, I believed things would improve despite not knowing the identity of the "voice." My best guess was that it was either my higher self or the Holy Spirit.

To my surprise, change wasn't four years away. In fact, my life turned around for the better in less than six months, even though I spent the summer grounded. But being grounded carried some benefits. It kept me away from my friends and out of trouble, as well as gave me time to reflect on my life. (Although my father caught me and my cousin stealing the family car.)

In 10th grade, I had an "ah-ha" moment while riding the school bus. I asked myself if I wanted to be smoking marijuana and partying five years from now. The answer was "no." Once more, the divine voice whispered to me, "Why don't you stop now?" I decided at that moment to leave smoking behind.

During my junior and senior years, I attended the vocational program for graphic design offered by my school district. It turned out to be one of the best decisions I made in school because it paved the way for my career path. I really enjoyed the center's independent learning approach and as a result, I graduated from high school with honors.

After graduation, I enrolled in the art program at our community college while working part-time as an ad designer for a local shopping guide.

When I was 23, a friend and co-worker loaned me the book *The Great Cosmic Mother* by Monica Sjoo and Barbara Mor. The book provided a detailed and well-researched exploration of all the religions since the beginning of time, starting with the worship of the Great Mother Goddess. It then delved into the pagan worshippers who were killed by the Christians and the resulting patriarchal system that eventually led to the infamous crusades and witch hunts.

Disillusioned by religion's history, I lost my faith in it. That would have been okay, but because I believed that God and religion were irrevocably intertwined, I also lost my belief in God. In hindsight, it wasn't a logical decision, but the religious dogma had been so firmly implanted in my mind that I couldn't separate God from religion.

A year and a half later, I met my soon-to-be husband, Jon Phillips (as of this writing, we've been married 30 years). We met through work. I loved working as a graphic designer there. My employer paid me well. I had flexible hours, worked with clients, figured out the profit and expenses for each project, and got paid on commission. At the end of the third year, I achieved my highest earnings to date, so I was blindsided during my performance review when my boss stated his intention to alter my commission structure, which would have resulted in a reduction of my annual pay by $12,000 (a value of $27,300 in today's economy). I was furious. He backed down, but the damage to the relationship had been done.

Because I couldn't go to another graphic design firm and still make the money I was making, it seemed my only option was to start my own company, but that was a risk.

To assess my ability to go solo, I compiled a list with the "pros" and "cons" categorized. Every night before going to sleep, I looked at the list, changing it when I figured out solutions to the problems listed on the "cons" side. Soon, the only problem listed was "lack of money." I remembered something my father once said to me, "If the only problem you have is lack of money, then you don't have a problem."

After several months of reviewing my list every night and envisioning my business as if it were already successful, I woke up with the unwavering knowledge it was time to start my business. I wasn't sure where this absolute knowledge came from, but it penetrated through all of my doubts.

I gave my two-week notice on Monday.

In my first year in business, I made 150 percent more than I did working at my old job, and my income continued to climb for many years.

Six years later, I had two small children, and my business continued to be successful. At that time, I read the book *The Four Agreements* by Don Miguel Ruiz, a best-seller and the closest thing to a metaphysical topic I had ever read. In his book, Ruiz mentioned he was a shaman in the Toltec tradition, the same as his mother. He grew up in Mexico and later became a neurosurgeon in the United States, but he soon realized that people created their illnesses, so he changed his field to psychology to better understand how people think. Then, he was involved in a car crash where he lifted the car off his brother. Ruiz's supernatural strength during a time of crisis prompted him to return to his shamanic upbringing. His story intrigued me, and I vowed that if I ever got the chance to learn more about shamanism (which I mistakenly believed was a Mexican religion), I would do so.

Oh, how the universe responds to our heartfelt vows. A few months later, I received a newsletter from a local hospital. Inside was a small ad promoting a six-week class on shamanism, so I signed up for it.

The first class went well. I sat and listened to the teacher talk about how indigenous tribes around the world practiced shamanism. She explained how shamans journeyed to the spirit realm to receive guidance, seek healing and connect with the universal powers. (For more information on shamanism, see the chapter at the back titled "Overview of Shamanism and Shamanic Journeying.")

The teacher seemed to be winding down for the night, so I grabbed my purse, thinking it was time to head out. However, the teacher announced it was time for us to shamanic journey. I was shocked. I had thought this class was a lecture series, not a workshop. Too embarrassed to leave, I stayed and shamanic journeyed. Much to my surprise, I discovered I had a natural ability for shamanic journeying, although I believed the spirit guides and totem animals I encountered were figments of my imagination.

A few weeks after completing the workshop, my family and I moved from Michigan to Tampa, Florida. I had no plans to continue to shamanic journey, but Pandora's Box had been opened. I had established a connection to the spirit realm, and every few weeks, my totem animals, spirit guides and ancestors would beckon me. I tried to ignore them, but their calls intensified the longer I ignored them. The only way I could shut them up was to shamanic journey. It was a strange disconnect between me not believing in a higher power and somehow understanding that "beings" were calling to me from the "other side."

A year later, my family and I moved to West Palm Beach. There, I saw an advertisement for an upcoming event at a local metaphysical bookstore. A man named William, who claimed to channel an enlightened being, offered a group reading.

Intrigued, I decided to attend. I found a good seat up front. William sat on a stool as he channeled. After an hour, most participants received a message for handling the realities of their lives. There were only a few people still waiting and I was worried William had overlooked me. I waited anxiously as William paused between messages and wondered who he would choose next.

Suddenly, he opened his eyes, pointed his finger at me, and loudly declared, "You are a healer!" I honestly looked behind myself, but when I turned back, he was still looking directly at me. Then he said, "One day you will be up here where I am, healing and teaching others." Although the message seemed ridiculous, the idea of being a healer tumbled through the back of my mind.

A few months later, "Jessica," who was a marketing director and one of my graphic design clients, was experiencing a mental breakdown due to her clinical depression and stressful work environment. She'd had other episodes in the previous years, and each one resulted in a minimum stay of a week at a psychiatric hospital while they reviewed her medications and sometimes performed electroshock treatments. It would then take her a week or two to recover at home. I thought, "Why not shamanic journey to request a healing for her? After all, I am supposed to be a healer."

Since it was the first time I had requested a healing, I asked my totem animal to show me the way. He led me to a spirit guide who accepted the healing request for Jessica. Instantly, the spirit guide and I were at the edge of Jessica's bed. The spirit guide symbolically opened up the top of her head and spun her brain. He called it a "spiritual lobotomy." I asked if he could do anything for her pain. He sprinkled a white powder inside her head and said, "Just a little something to take the edge off." I thanked him for doing the healing, but still, the vision did not seem real.

The following day I called Jessica's office, expecting to speak with her assistant, but was pleasantly surprised to hear Jessica's voice on the phone. When I expressed my surprise, she responded that she was, too. She told me earlier that morning she and her therapist had tried to analyze why she woke up feeling so good, but she couldn't think of anything she had done that would have contributed to easing her depression.

To discover if my healing request had led to Jessica's healing or if it was a coincidence, I continued asking for healing for other people. Over several months, I observed people being healed, although I remained uncertain whether my healing requests were the catalysts or simply coincidental. I had yet to return to my faith in God, so I was understandably confused and doubtful about the healings. After each one, I convinced myself the healing requests weren't an integral part of the process, yet I also felt compelled to keep making them. My doubts fought against me every step of the way.

Around this time, my husband, Jon, became ill. We rushed him to the emergency room with severe pain in his lower abdomen and later admitted him to the hospital. But after four days, an MRI scan and a team of doctors working on him, he was sent home with no diagnosis. However, he kept having painful attacks, and each time, he was rushed back to the emergency room. The medical bills were stacking up fast, and the doctors still didn't have an answer. Finally, a nurse quietly told us in the emergency room that Jon had the symptoms of Crohn's disease and to see a specialist.

The nurse was right, and my husband was diagnosed with Crohn's, which is an incurable, chronic illness that causes extreme pain in the lower intestinal tract.

After a few months of debilitating pain and excessive weight loss, I asked Jon if I could perform a healing for him despite my own doubts about the shamanic healing process. To my surprise, he agreed to take part in the healing. However, I wasn't sure if he was humoring me or willing to try anything at that point.

We lay on our bed while I shamanic journeyed. A spirit guide appeared as a Native American medicine man. The spirit guide sucked the sickness from my husband's intestines and spit it into a fire that burned in a stone bowl. After the spirit guide finished the healing, he gave me the results — my husband would be well in two weeks.

Just as the spirit guides had professed, my husband was better within the given time frame and began looking for work. (Jon has remained symptom-free to this day.) It was truly a miracle.

Until this point, I had been performing healings through shamanic journeying as an atheist, which I guess proves you don't have to believe in something for it to be true, but after a few years of healing others, I wanted to know where the power came from. This thought persistently nagged me for weeks. Then my mother called. As we discussed the healings I had been a part of, she asked, "Where do you think God fits into all this?"

I replied that if God was part of the healings, He certainly was more than capable of showing Himself. As I said this, an energetic pressure began pushing down on the top of my head and flowing through my body. It became so intense that I couldn't lift my head. I was literally resting my head on the desk, trying to talk. Finally, I said, "Mom, I'm going to have to call you back," and ran to my room to shamanic journey.

During the shamanic journey, I was led to a realm where Jesus Christ stood to greet me. I was stunned. As a kid, I often talked with Jesus, but it had been so long since I thought of Him or even believed He existed. Now He stood before me with welcoming arms. There was no judgment or condemnation for my lack of faith. Overwhelmed with joy, I walked towards Him.

Jesus said, "Welcome back. We have so much to do. Together, we can heal. You remember all the healings that I performed while on earth. Together, you and I can do so much more."

Although I was happy that Jesus had returned to my life, I was skeptical of being able to heal on a full-time basis. So I said, "Well, I can't pull gold coins out of fish's mouths like you can. I have to work for a living."

Instead of judging my smart-aleck remark, Jesus smiled and said, "Hold out your hand." And I did. He placed two gold coins in my palm. "I will take care of you. Go and do what needs to be done."

Despite this interaction, I still didn't believe in God.

Six months later, mainly because the economy had taken a turn for the worse in 2007, and partly because I'm not a great salesperson, my graphic design business was no longer sustaining me. On top of that, my husband and I were upside down on five of our investment properties because of the housing collapse, which forced us to declare bankruptcy. It felt like I was reliving my parent's bankruptcy, which was also caused by a recession and housing market collapse.

For financial reasons, I accepted a position as a graphic designer at a mid-size company. Taking this job meant admitting the business I had owned for 16 years — one that had been very lucrative until recently — was officially closed.

Perhaps because I needed comfort or because I had asked God to show himself months earlier while talking with my mother, I was about to experience one of the greatest miracles of my life.

The miracle occurred while I was showering in the octagon-shaped, walk-in shower in our beautiful house from which we would soon be evicted. Each angled wall held a half-moon window that offered a panoramic view of the blue sky and white, fluffy clouds.

I was shampooing my hair when I looked out one of the shower windows and saw the face of God! It was perfect. It was as if an artist had chiseled God's face out of a solid block of cloud. Every detail was there: hair, eyebrows, eyes, nose, mouth, and even a mustache and beard. I stood there, stunned. One part of me was in awe of the miracle, and another part of me thought how perfectly natural it felt to see God. I stood there staring until the shampoo began running down my face. I turned to rinse the shampoo, but when I looked back, only a few remnants of God's beard and hair remained. It was as if a giant hand had wiped the face away.

Immediately, doubt set in. My mind rationalized that while there might be a billion-to-one chance of God's face appearing in perfect detail, it could have been a natural phenomenon. Yet the other part of my mind was saying, "It would have to be a completely calm day to have that kind of detail appear, yet the face was 'blown away' in a few seconds... Why shouldn't God appear?... He's capable of anything!"

My mind went back and forth from awe to doubt as I massaged conditioner into my hair. Then I looked out one of the other shower windows and was shocked to see God's face staring at me for a second time! It looked *exactly* like the first one. I glanced back to the other window and could still see the remnants of the first face there. Even my logical mind couldn't deny this one. I turned back to gaze at God's face, realizing He had given me a sign I could not dispute.

Seeing God's face erased any doubt I had of His existence and proved to me He is more than capable of showing Himself.

Finally, I turned away to rinse the conditioner out of my hair. When I looked back, the second face had also been brushed away. And just like the first one, only a few wispy remnants remained as evidence of the miracle.

A year later, I felt the Spirit calling me to leave Florida despite my love for the state. The only problem was that I wasn't sure where that other place was.

My husband and I both quit our jobs in July 2008 and used our tax refund to fund a two-week road trip. We planned to visit cities in North Carolina, Georgia and Virginia, as well as Michigan, where our families lived.

The road trip would offer me lots of time to read in the minivan, so I searched for books to bring along. However, nothing in the bookstores stood out and I had read everything in the house except for one book, *A Course in Miracles*. My father had given me the book several years earlier, but I had only read the first page, which said, "All miracles mean life, and God is the Giver of life." When I saw the word "God," I stopped reading and put the book back on the shelf where it had been sitting ever since, collecting dust. However, my viewpoint on God had changed since then. And although I believed ACIM was a textbook for a theology college course, I was willing to read it to see how it claimed miracles occurred and compare its thought process to shamanism.

It turned out that ACIM was not a college textbook. Instead, I learned the writings were channeled and written in shorthand by Helen Schucman, and put into words by William Thetford, both professors at Columbia University's College of Physicians and Surgeons in New York City. The channeling was a strange occurrence to have happened to an atheist.

The book was written in Shakespearean verse and difficult to comprehend, but riding in the minivan provided the perfect situation for absorbing the complex reading material. I would read a few paragraphs or a page at a time and aimlessly gaze at the passing landscape while my brain processed the teachings. Once the message was digested, I would resume reading again, and sometimes be completely immersed in the message and hear its "voice" talking to me.

I was surprised that I could find nothing in ACIM that contradicted shamanism. In fact, its teachings added valuable insight into how shamanic healing occurs. For example, ACIM teaches that there are spiritual teachers, such as Jesus and others, who provide guidance to those of us who are still in human form. In shamanism, these teachers would be called spirit guides.

ACIM speaks of miracles altering the past to heal the present and thereby changing the future. I had already seen how shamanic healing could cut karmic ties to people's pasts to heal their present lives.

ACIM teaches that through forgiveness, we remove the blockages from our minds that keep us from knowing our spiritual selves and achieving wholeness. In shamanism, shamans perform soul retrievals to search and retrieve lost soul parts to heal and restore the soul to wholeness. Whether you call it blockages or lost soul parts, both have the same goal of wholeness.

After our travels, my family and I decided to move to the Raleigh, North Carolina, metro area because it was home to hundreds of corporate headquarters and seemed like an ideal place to raise a family.

My husband saw a shooting star the night before we moved and mentioned that he hadn't seen one in years.

The next evening, we headed off to Jacksonville, Florida, where we would spend the night before continuing to North Carolina. As we pulled into the hotel parking lot, a shooting star fell over the hotel — it felt like we were following guiding stars.

A few weeks after our move, while I was driving home at night from *A Course in Miracles* gathering, I thought how crazy it had been to move to a different state based on psychic readings. Especially since neither my husband nor I had jobs lined up and we were living off our mutual funds.

I remembered how the shooting stars had shown themselves at the beginning of our move, but neither my husband nor I had seen one since we arrived in North Carolina. Panic started to set in, so I asked the Holy Spirit for a sign, "Please show me a shooting star if this is where I am supposed to be right now."

Immediately, a shooting star appeared! But it fell along the edge of a grain silo, and I wondered if maybe it had been a headlight reflection (there was no limit to my ego's ability to cast doubt). So I asked the Divine to send me a second shooting star. As soon as I finished the request, a shooting star fell in the middle of the night sky. Finally, there was no doubt in my mind that this was where I was supposed to be. And as I traveled down the road, the streetlights flickered off, one by one.

Fast-forward 16 years. I was still living in North Carolina, wondering how to move forward spiritually and financially and what "moving forward" even meant. I felt misaligned with the universe.

I expected to be further along on my life's journey, especially since I had experienced so many major life shifts in my life. It had been a roller coaster ride from poverty to abundance and back again. I was raised in a bi-racial home, lived in the city and country, and moved from the north to the south. I had lost my faith in Christianity, became an atheist, and then discovered shamanism, which led to miracles and renewed my faith in God.

Despite my diverse, incredible and sometimes traumatic experiences, I realized there was still much to learn about leading a spiritual life aligned with God's

Will while achieving the prosperity I desired. I wanted answers on how to move forward.

As a shamanic healer, I often relied on my spirit guides to provide physical and spiritual healing, but I hesitated to ask them how to achieve abundance or for advice on practical matters. On the rare occasions when I did ask them, their answers were vague or focused on the spiritual aspects of the questions.

I wondered if changing my views on receiving more specific answers would affect the ability of the spirit guides to answer my questions in a more specific manner. I also wondered what the Course had to say about changing this Dream. Was changing my part of the Dream to suit my preferences worthwhile, or was that promoting duality?

I did some research and came across this verse in the URtext of *A Course in Miracles*: "Choose your questions wisely, meaning the more limits imposed in your question, the more limited your response from the Creative powers will be."

The question limits the answer.

If the question is so important, how do I know what to ask for? Without divine guidance, how could I be sure that what I wanted was in my best interest mentally, physically, financially and spiritually? How could I be sure my plans, no matter how well-planned or logical, wouldn't topple into a giant mess? Or worse, waste my time reaching for the next shiny object only to discover it was a diversion created by my ego.

Was anything worth pursuing? I felt there must be. Surely I couldn't be expected to sit under a tree waiting for enlightenment. Or maybe I could. The Course has an entire section titled "I Need Do Nothing," yet I felt the need to do something.

I wanted to know if altering the Dream was a desirable pursuit, so I asked the Holy Spirit and Jesus to inspire me in this endeavor to discover the answers to my questions so I could help myself and others. This book is the outcome of that exploration.

Overview of the Miraculous Life Process

"Every time you choose love over fear, you

perform a miracle."

You are Always Altering the Dream

You are deciding every moment of every day, and every decision you make reflects whether you are listening to your ego or the Holy Spirit. Whichever voice you listen to influences your thoughts, and because thoughts contain energy, they impact your life.

When your thoughts are aligned with God's love, your thoughts create what is in your best interest. When your thoughts are aligned with your ego, you create experiences that cause needless suffering for yourself and others.

"Whatever you accept into your mind has reality for you. It is your acceptance of it that makes it real. If you enthrone the ego in your mind, your allowing it to enter makes it your reality. This is because the mind is capable of creating reality or making illusions. I said before that you must learn to think with God. To think with Him is to think like Him. This engenders joy, not guilt, because it is natural." T-5.V.4:1-7

If you are not *intentionally* manifesting your life, you are choosing to accept the Dream as it was originally created, either because you do not recognize your power to manifest a new reality for yourself or you are listening to the lies of the ego.

You have the option to alter your destiny because it is not etched in stone. Your destiny is like a cosmic blueprint for a house under construction. You have the ability to make changes, knock out walls, add new features, change the colors and so on. You don't have to accept poor-quality workmanship. You can build a mansion for yourself or a quaint cottage in the woods, depending on your preference.

Since most people do not believe their thoughts can change their lives, they feel like victims of this Dream, caught up in the waves that keep bashing them against the rocks — but they always have a choice.

One of the most difficult aspects of starting the Miraculous Life Process will be admitting you have manifested everything that has happened in your life. It might seem like you've made a lot of mistakes and there may be things you feel guilty about, but this process isn't about blaming you or anyone else. It's about picking up where you are right now and moving forward in the direction you want to go. It's about self-empowerment.

To chart your course, you must admit you're the navigator. Once you do this, you will access the incredible power within yourself and the Creative powers to steer your life in your chosen direction. If you add to this process by manifesting with the Holy Spirit's guidance and power, you will create a life that goes beyond mere abundance for yourself — you will create a life overflowing with miracles.

> "It is impossible that anything should come to me unbidden by myself. Even in this world, it is I who rule my destiny. What happens is what I desire. What does not occur is what I do not want to happen. This must I accept." W-pII.253.1.1-5

> "This is the only thing that you need do for vision, happiness, release from pain and the complete escape from sin, all to be given you. Say only this, but mean it with no reservations, for here the power of salvation lies: I **am** responsible for what I see. I choose the feelings I experience, and I decide upon the goal I would achieve. And everything that seems to happen to me I ask for, and receive as I have asked." T-21.II.2.1-5

The Creative powers recognize all of your requests, whether they are positive and loving or negative and unloving. You might ask yourself, "Why would I create experiences I don't want?" Well, the answer is threefold.

First, you didn't know about the universal laws of cause and effect, which means you were unaware of your role in creating your unwanted experiences as well as your capacity to shape the events in your life.

Second, you exist within an ancient Dream that was dreamed so long ago that you have no memory of its beginning, but you perceive it as if it is happening now. When you accept the Dream in its original state, you pave the way for pre-existing events to unfold, which may include some undesirable experiences. However, with the Holy Spirit's help, you could heal your portion of the Dream, potentially preventing undesirable aspects from unfolding and allowing a better reality to take its place.

> "It is impossible the Son of God be merely driven by events outside of him. It is impossible that happenings that come to him were not his choice. His power of decision is the determiner of every situation in which he seems to find himself by chance or accident. No accident nor chance is possible within the universe as God created it, outside of which is nothing. Suffer, and you decided sin was your goal. Be happy, and you gave the power of decision to Him Who must decide for God for you." T-21.II.3.1-6

Third, some of your manifestation requests may not materialize because your spirit knows that a specific lesson has not yet been learned and it deems the lesson to be more important than your request.

We should all be grateful that God has blessed us with the incredible gift of being able to make choices that shape our lives, even if some of those decisions are made at a spiritual level. However, as humans, we often make faulty decisions when relying solely on ourselves. Fortunately, we can seek guidance from the Holy Spirit, Jesus and divine helpers whenever we need it.

Everyone has created the life they lead and everyone can re-create it. There are no victims of fate here. We dictate what we experience in life because our thoughts create our world.

It is possible for everyone to have all they need. So why don't they? Why don't you? Why don't I? Our beliefs are limiting our lives.

Envision Your Future as If It is True Now

When you visualize your heart's desires, seeing them as if they were already true now is extremely important because the Creative powers respond to your visualizations based on your beliefs. If you believe your heart's desires are somewhere in the distant future, then they will always be out of reach in the distant future.

You can read more about this in the "Envision the Future as If It is Happening Now" chapter.

Thoughts are More Powerful than Actions

We have been taught to believe that hard work is the path to success, but our actions cannot outweigh our thoughts, because thoughts are the most powerful force in the universe. It seems backward, doesn't it? But those who work back-breaking jobs are seldom the wealthiest members of society. Hard work is not enough.

Your thoughts are the catalysts that prompt the Creative powers to usher in your life's experiences — for better or worse.

Because your thoughts attract matching experiences into your life, it's extremely important for you to focus only on what you want. For example, when struggling to pay your bills, it's easy to focus on not having enough money, but that is exactly what you should *not* do because whatever you think about will cause you to attract more of the same. Instead, focus on what you truly desire, such as financial freedom.

The more often you think about a specific experience you want to have in your life, the more powerful your thoughts become about that intended experience — and the more likely it will occur.

It might be hard to believe that thoughts produce physical energy, but science uses this fact with amazing results to help people, such as amputees who wear robotic prosthetics with sensors that interpret their brain impulses.

I once played a game called Mindflex, which allowed me to experience the power of my thoughts. To play, I had to wear an EEG headband connected to a base that released air, propelling a small plastic ball upwards. The more I focused on raising the ball, the stronger the airflow became and the ball would go higher. However, the ball would fall back onto the base as soon as I stopped concentrating. This game clearly demonstrated the tangible energy of thoughts.

Here's an analogy of how your thoughts impact your life. Imagine yourself waiting at a train station. You are sitting on a bench, contemplating your idea. As your idea takes shape, you enjoy visualizing it as *if it were already happening in the present moment.* As your idea becomes clearer and more refined, your confidence and focus grow, enhancing its potential and eliciting feelings of anticipation.

The combination of focused thought and strong emotion attracts the attention of the universal conductor, who pulls a train into the station. You get on board and take a seat.

The train moves ahead, and your thoughts increase in power as you become passionate about your idea. Out of the windows, you see new towns and different landscapes that inspire you to expand on your idea, and you become more enthused about reaching your destination. The train speeds up. Your thoughts and emotions act as fuel for the rest of the journey.

When you reach your destination, you step off the train to meet the opportunities waiting for you, and then you take the inspired action necessary to bring your idea to life.

Time Has a Safety Valve

Our universe has a "safety valve" that acts as a time delay, which prevents your thoughts from manifesting immediately (except in cases of miracles). This allows you time to correct your thoughts if necessary. So don't fear new ideas, because they won't manifest instantly.

The Holy Spirit Can Alter Time

When a certain lesson in the Dream is learned, the Holy Spirit collapses the parts of the Dream that are no longer necessary. This allows us to avoid being trapped in the Dream for thousands or even millions of years, thus saving us time.

> "Delay does not matter in eternity, but it is tragic in time." T-5.VI.1.3

There is more on the subject of time in the "Time Can Work for You" chapter.

The Divine is Always Communicating with Us

The Divine is always speaking to us, although we seldom hear it because of the random thoughts rambling around our minds. However, in moments of silence, we can hear the Divine when our minds are still. Fortunately, when it's extremely important, the Divine will flow between the gaps in our thoughts to communicate with us vividly.

Once, when my husband and I were in the process of purchasing our house, we planned to use the money from the IRA I had inherited from my late mother. In hindsight, I realize I should have removed the funds immediately after we signed the contract, but unfortunately, I didn't consider the possibility of a stock market fluctuation.

Just a few days before the house's scheduled closing, I was running an errand. I had just pulled into the parking lot when the Divine suddenly told me I needed to withdraw my money that day, but it was already 4:00 p.m.

After rushing home, I promptly accessed the website. Honestly, I was surprised I even found the password. In addition, because I had never withdrawn money from this investment account before, I had to read the instructions. Time was ticking away. I finally completed my withdrawal request, only to see a tax form pop up on the screen. I hurriedly filled it out and submitted it. I finished at 4:58 p.m.

The next trading day, the stock market crashed so severely that they named it Black Monday 2011. If I hadn't taken out the money when I did, I wouldn't have had the money I needed to buy the house. Fortunately, the Divine has much more common sense than I do and knowledge of future events.

I was blessed to have such clear divine guidance, which is not always the case. Divine guidance is usually more subtle, appearing as whispers, gut feelings or passing thoughts. Still, no matter how the Divine communicates with us, it can be a regular part of our lives, especially when we seek guidance.

Emotions Act as a Barometer

Often, we believe our intellect is the key to making excellent decisions. We downplay our emotions as irrational, but emotions are an important way the Holy Spirit, Jesus and divine helpers communicate with us.

When you have a concern, take the time to ask the Divine to help you understand what is wrong with the current situation. Then, pay attention to the emotions that come to you. The Divine can speak to you through your heart. When you pay attention to how you feel about a decision, you will more easily navigate life and avoid the more significant problems that might develop because you ignored the early warning signs.

> "When your mood tells you that you have chosen wrongly, and this is so whenever you are not joyous, then *know this need not be.* In every case you have thought wrongly about some brother God created, and are perceiving images your ego makes in a darkened glass. Think honestly what you have thought that God would not have thought, and what you have not thought that God would have you think. Search sincerely for what you have done and left undone accordingly, and then change your mind to think with God's." T-4.IV.2.2-5

Later in this book, there is a chapter and exercise on using emotions as a barometer.

When You Gain, Everyone Gains

When working with the Holy Spirit, you will not have to worry about whether your desires are selfish because the Holy Spirit will lead you along a path where everyone benefits.

> "Miracles are selective only in the sense that they are directed towards those who can use them for themselves. Since this makes it inevitable that they

will extend them to others, a strong chain of Atonement is welded." T-1.III.9.1-2

A deep connection binds us all together on an energetic level. Each of us is like a wave in the ocean, cresting towards the sun, and it is impossible for us not to affect others as we ebb and flow through life. By being in a state of happiness, good health and financial abundance, you elevate the overall vibrance of humanity.

When you co-create with the Holy Spirit, as opposed to following your ego's plan or relying solely on your own thought processes, your requests are fulfilled in a way that benefits everyone. Only the Holy Spirit fully knows the future and what truly benefits you.

> "The Holy Spirit offers you release from every problem that you think you have. They are the same to Him because each one, regardless of the form it seems to take, is a demand that someone suffer loss and make a sacrifice that you might gain. And when the situation is worked out so no one loses is the problem gone, because it was an error in perception that now has been corrected." T-26.II.2:1-3

Ask and You Will Receive

The power of Free Will allows you to make your own choices. The Holy Spirit respects your autonomy and will never impose anything on you that you are unwilling to receive. To get what you want, ask for it. When you do, it shows you are open to receiving it.

The Holy Spirit welcomes all requests because it wants to be an integral part of your life. When you act on your own, you are deciding to keep certain aspects of your life separate from the Holy Spirit. This leaves an opening for your ego to misguide you.

The Holy Spirit always responds to your requests, although its answers may not always meet your expectations. But you don't have to worry that the Holy Spirit's responses will result in more loss than gain for you. The Holy Spirit, with a complete understanding of your preferences and life's lessons, only desires what is best for you.

"You may complain that this course is not sufficiently specific for you to understand and use. Yet perhaps you have not done what it specifically advocates. This is not a course in the play of ideas, but in their practical application. Nothing could be more specific than to be told that if you ask you will receive. The Holy Spirit will answer every specific problem as long as you believe that problems are specific. His answer is both many and one, as long as you believe that the one is many. You may be afraid of His specificity, for fear of what you think it will demand of you. Yet only by asking will you learn that nothing of God demands anything of you. God gives; He does not take. When you refuse to ask, it is because you believe that asking is taking rather than sharing." T-11.VIII.5.1-10

Release Your Blockages for Maximum Benefits

When you take steps to heal and release your negative emotions and thoughts, you remove the blockages between you and the Creative powers, opening up the gateway to receive your heart's desires.

The chapter "Release the Blockages to Abundance" provides additional information about this topic, followed by a practical exercise.

Take Action When You Feel Inspired

The final and crucial step in the Miraculous Life Process is for you to take action based on the guidance, inspiration and opportunities you received because of your consistent heartfelt requests to the divine power. Your thoughts are more powerful than your actions, but inspired action is a necessary step.

Time Can Work for You

"Time seems to go in one direction, but when you reach its end it will roll up like a long carpet spread along the past behind you, and will disappear." T-13.I.3.5

You Have All the Time You Need

If you worry about not having enough time, you will strengthen your belief in its scarcity. And because the Creative powers honor your beliefs, you won't have enough time.

Instead of worrying about a lack of time, trust that your inspired ideas wouldn't have been given to you if you didn't have enough time to either fulfill them or embark on a worthwhile journey.

"Can you imagine what it means to have no cares, no worries, no anxieties, but merely to be perfectly calm and quiet all the time? Yet that is what time is for; to learn just that and nothing more." T-15.I.1.1-2

Protective Time Delay

The presence of a time delay within the Dream serves as a safety valve that prevents your thoughts from instantly changing the trajectory of your life. Think about all the times you shouted, "I wish you were dead!" or "I hate my job so much that I wish they'd fire me." Thank God for the time delay!

The time delay allows you to reevaluate your thoughts and think of new ones before your misguided thoughts can affect your life. But on the flip side, because of the time delay, things often take longer to change than you would like, increasing the likelihood of you giving up too soon.

The Holy Spirit's Alteration of Time

I've always been fascinated by the Course's teachings about the Holy Spirit's ability to alter time. According to Albert Einstein, time is relative, but the Course claims it can also be abolished and collapsed, accelerating our awakening.

> "The miracle minimizes the need for time. In the longitudinal or horizontal plane the recognition of the equality of the members of the Sonship appears to involve almost endless time. However, the miracle entails a sudden shift from horizontal to vertical

perception. This introduces an interval from which the giver and receiver both emerge farther along in time than they would otherwise have been. The miracle thus has the unique property of abolishing time to the extent that it renders the interval of time it spans unnecessary. There is no relationship between the time a miracle takes and the time it covers. The miracle substitutes for learning that might have taken thousands of years. It does so by the underlying recognition of perfect equality of giver and receiver on which the miracle rests. The miracle shortens time by collapsing it, thus eliminating certain intervals within it. It does this, however, within the larger temporal sequence." T-1.II.6.1-10

When the Holy Spirit heals our lives, we often won't know that time has collapsed or been abolished because some of our future events no longer need to play out, but sometimes we can see the effects of time being altered.

One of those times occurred while I was driving home late one night from a friend's house. I had called my sister to stay awake while driving on the lonely highway. She lived out West, so while it was close to midnight in North Carolina, it was only 9:00 p.m. in Nevada. We talked for ten minutes before she suddenly became extremely nauseous. She said it was odd since she had been fine all day. She needed to end the call, so we said goodbye, and I set my phone on the seat.

A few minutes later, I drove over a hill and saw a herd of deer crossing the divided highway in front of me. I looked in every direction for a path to avoid them, but there was no visible escape route. I remember thinking, "There is no way I won't hit those deer!" I expected to hit not just one, but several deer, and I went limp, surrendering to the inevitable.

Suddenly, my body had a mind of its own. A presence took control of me and slammed my foot on the brakes, filling the night air with the sound of screeching tires.

Time began to move in slow motion, and as I passed the buck on my left, I looked into his wide eyes staring back at me. He was so close that I watched the side-view mirror miss his antlers by inches. When he was safely out of the way, my hand cranked the wheel sharply to the left to dodge the deer on my right, which kindly took several steps in the opposite direction to avoid being hit.

Now, I was driving on the bumpy, grassy median and about to plow into another deer before me when my hand swerved the wheel back to the right, narrowly missing the doe.

Safely back on the highway, I looked in the rearview mirror to see the deer still standing there, stunned. The two cars in front of me had their brakes on, no doubt wondering if they would need to stop and call 911, but when they saw me putter along the highway unharmed, their brake lights went off and everyone resumed driving.

Time returned to normal and I assessed what had just occurred. Unscathed, I first thanked God for saving the deer's lives. Then, another mile down the road, I realized that I could have been killed and thanked Him for saving mine.

The following day, my sister called. She mentioned her nausea had passed within a few minutes after hanging up the phone the night before. I realized that if we had still been on the phone, I wouldn't have been paying full attention to my driving nor had two hands on the wheel when I drove through the herd of deer. I considered her nausea to be the work of divine intervention. (Please don't judge me for holding a phone while driving. I was driving an older model Dodge Durango after our bankruptcy. There was no hands-free option on that baby, and the hands-free law in North Carolina didn't pass until nearly a decade later.)

The Divine had altered time and allowed me to drive through a herd of deer unharmed, using its extraordinary ability to slow time. Once we understand that the past, present and future all exist simultaneously, our comprehension expands to include the idea that all timelines are malleable. Because of the power we are working with, have faith that you will receive miracles.

Chapter Questions

Take a moment to reflect on this chapter, and then write down your personal thoughts and insights to the following questions.

1. Remember a time when you felt a sense of urgency or scarcity around time. How did this belief impact your experience?

2. Can you recall a moment when a delay in your plans or desires proved to be a blessing in disguise? How did this delay offer you an opportunity for reflection or redirection?

____

____

____

____

____

____

____

3. How does the idea of collapsing time resonate with you, and can you recall any personal experiences where time seemed to bend or shift unexpectedly?

____

____

---

4.   Reflect on a moment in your life where you felt
     guided or protected by a force beyond your
     understanding. How did this experience deepen
     your trust in the divine timing of events?

You Can Use Emotions as a Barometer

"Nothing great was ever achieved without enthusiasm." Ralph Waldo Emerson

Using your emotions as a guidance tool is a great way to start the Miraculous Life Process because you've noticed whether you are sad or happy, afraid or empowered, excited or hesitant your whole life. You won't have to learn a whole new system to manifest the life you want — you will just have to learn to pay more attention to whether your emotions feel desirable or undesirable.

To discover if you are on the right track, tell the Holy Spirit or Jesus your plans. As you speak, pay attention to how you feel. Do you feel drawn to go a different way than originally planned? Sometimes, a plan is good, but the timing isn't right and you feel the hesitation. And sometimes, the plan isn't right for *you*. Pay attention to how you feel when asking for guidance. Emotions that align with feeling "right" are happiness, anticipation, enthusiasm, joy, etc. Emotions that accompany feeling "wrong" are confusion, doubt, fear, hesitation, etc.

If you feel a negative emotion while envisioning your idea, experiment with it. Maybe the timeline or intentions aren't quite right. Finesse your idea to see if you can get it to a point where your heart sends you positive emotions. If your idea still doesn't feel right after all of that visualization, it might be time to go back to the drawing board or wait for a better time.

Don't Let Fear Derail You

Keep in mind that emotions have the potential to be deceiving because your ego can spin a web of lies and fear in your mind. So what was a good idea, may now frighten you.

In addition, it is crucial to recognize that making choices that benefit your own personal growth may involve confronting your fears. Fear is often present in your most significant moments, like purchasing a new house or saying, "I love you," for the first time.

Your ego, which thrives on chaos and fear, is particularly prone to attacking you when you are making harmonious decisions. By following your heart and pushing past your fears, you open yourself up to a multitude of rewarding experiences that will enrich your life.

"The ego is, therefore, particularly likely to attack you when you react lovingly, because it has evaluated you as unloving and you are going against its judgment. The ego will attack your motives as soon as they become clearly out of accord with its perception of you." T-9.VII.4.5-6

The Course talks a great deal about fear, but Jesus said fear is not real.

"Nothing and everything cannot coexist. To believe in one is to deny the other. Fear is really nothing and love is everything. Whenever light enters darkness, the darkness is abolished." T-2.VII.5.1-4

The way you handle fear is what really counts. Although it is common to experience fear before important events, it is crucial to recognize that fear should not prevent you from moving forward. Rather than focusing on your fear, consider whether the choice aligns with your heart by asking yourself, "Despite my fear, does this *feel* like the right path?"

Jesus recommended that we ask Him for guidance so we can feel confident in our decisions and eliminate our fear.

"The correction of fear *is* your responsibility. When you ask for release from fear, you are implying that it is not. You should ask, instead, for help in the conditions that have brought the fear about. These conditions always entail a willingness to be separate. At that level you *can* help it. You are much too tolerant of mind wandering, and are passively condoning your mind's miscreations. The particular result does not matter, but the fundamental error does. The correction is always the same. Before you choose to do anything, ask me if your choice is in accord with mine. If you are sure that it is, there will be no fear." T-2.VI.4.1-10

Chapter Questions

Take a moment to reflect on this chapter, and then write down your personal thoughts and insights to the following questions.

1. Remember a situation where you noticed your emotions and were able to shift them purposely. How did this emotional change influence the situation?

____

____

____

____

____

____

____

____

2. Consider a time when you felt hesitant or
    doubtful about a decision or plan. How did these
    negative emotions impact your willingness to
    move forward?

____

____

____

____

____

____

3. How do you distinguish between fear that serves as a warning sign and fear that arises from ego-based illusions? Share any strategies you intend to use to navigate through your fears and align with your true desires.

____

____

____

____

____

4. Reflect on how your heart and higher self play a role in your decision-making. How do you recognize when your intuition is guiding you toward a path that aligns with your highest good? Describe any experiences where you felt a strong sense of inner knowing despite external doubts or fears.

____

____

----

5. Describe an experience where fear or discomfort ultimately led to personal expansion and transformation in your life. Reflect on any insights gained from overcoming your fear as a catalyst for growth and evolution.

Release the Blockages to Abundance

"I say 'Out' to every negative thought that comes to my mind. No person, place, or thing has any power over me, for I am the only thinker in my mind. I create my own reality and everyone in it." Louise Hay

Negative thoughts and emotions from your past can sabotage your relationships, finances, peace of mind and health by creating blockages between you and the Creative powers.

Like most of my life's lessons, I learned the importance of releasing the blockages the hard way.

The course of events started one morning while I was sitting at my computer and, from out of nowhere, I had my first and only panic attack. When it hit, I rushed out of the room, trying to outrun the fear. With my heart pounding, I stopped at the top of the stairs and prayed to the Holy Spirit, "I don't want to feel this way! Please take it and heal it!" and then I stepped down the stairs. By the time I reached the bottom step, the panic attack had passed. I was impressed by how quickly the Holy Spirit had healed me, especially since this was the first time I had asked the Holy Spirit for a healing without shamanic journeying.

Shortly after this healing, my mother died unexpectedly. She was riding a bicycle when a car hit her. As tragic as her death was, her spirit returned to offer me my greatest miracle.

As soon as I got the horrific news of my mother's passing, my family and I drove through the night from North Carolina to Michigan. I sobbed the entire way. We arrived on Sunday afternoon, just in time to eat an early dinner with my immediate family. Afterward, my siblings and I felt compelled to visit our mother's house and choose the clothes she would wear in her casket.

On our way to her house, we passed the accident scene. My brother slowed down and asked if I wanted to see it. My chest tightened even more, but I said, "Yes."

Fluorescent orange, spray-painted marks covered the road and adjacent grassy slope. Each one marked relevant evidence of the collision... a piece of a headlight here and a side-view mirror there. A circle painted around a gouge in the asphalt pavement showed the point of impact. My brother explained the markings and finally pointed to the spot on the grassy slope where our mother had landed after being thrown from the impact. Orange letters indicated the position of her head, body and legs. How do you deal with something like this? I crouched down and touched the grass. Anger burst forth and I thought, *Why did you leave me, Mom!?*

Tuesday morning, my husband and I went to my mother's workplace to meet with the HR director at the state department where my mother had worked for 32 years. My sister met us there.

The HR director got to the business at hand. She informed us that our mother's accounts would be divided equally among her three children, but the pension would be given solely to my sister. Immediately, I resented that my sister was given the entire pension, especially since my family was struggling financially, but I didn't want to feel this way.

Following the meeting, the HR director escorted us to our mother's cubicle to clean it out. I was emotionally distant from my sister as we emptied the drawers.

I kept battling the resentment that stabbed at me by repeatedly asking the Holy Spirit to take this anger from me.

Suddenly, my mother's spirit descended over me and her vision became mine. I felt her glasses resting on the bridge of my nose. Through her eyes, the entire world glowed with love. The office building and the world beyond disappeared into a golden light and I felt all the souls in Creation pulsating through me. When I looked at my sister, rays of light radiated from her. Her body was barely visible and I saw her soul in the center of her chest, smiling back at me. Her soul, which looked like a friendly ghost with an oversized head and small nondescript body, gave me a shy smile that seemed to say, "You found me."

> "The Great Rays would establish the total lack of value of the special relationship, if they were seen. For in seeing them the body would disappear, because its value would be lost." T-16.VI.4.5-6

My mother's memories filled my consciousness and I could see my sister as the little girl, teenager and young woman she had raised. My mother saw her as an innocent daughter who would be taken care of with the pension she had inherited. I felt the comfort that it gave my mother and the love she had for my sister. Immediately, all resentment left me. I knew my mother had given the pension out of love, and as I experienced that love, it became impossible for me to feel anything else.

Then my mother was gone.

My mother had given me several beautiful gifts. First, she comforted me with the knowledge of her undying love and immersed her spirit with mine, and, for a moment, I saw my sister through her vision of all-encompassing love, which healed my heart. In addition, I knew the Holy Spirit had worked with my mother to provide me with a glimpse into heaven where I felt the love of all the souls in Creation. It was the only moment in my life that I felt was truly real.

The astounding experience showed me that I did not have to be pure in my heart to receive miracles. I only had to be willing to ask for healing, and then allow the

Divine's loving light to dissolve the darkness in my mind and heart.

> "The necessary condition for the holy instant does not require that you have no thoughts that are not pure. But it does require that you have none that you would keep." T-15.IV.9.1-2

A year after the miraculous experience with my mother's spirit, my husband and I pursued buying a house using the settlement money from my mother's wrongful death lawsuit. We had to pay cash because of our bankruptcy after the housing crash in 2007. Our choices were very limited because of our budget, but one house stood out. It was a HUD foreclosure that had been vacant for more than a year and vandalized by the neighborhood teenagers. Since no one else had shown an interest in the property, we made a low-ball offer, which HUD countered, and we countered again, but someone swooped in and outbid us.

Losing a bid on a house that had been on the market for nearly a year was the final straw. I knew I needed to let go of the past to end this nonstop cycle of always losing out on the abundance the universe is so willing to give to all of us.

So I spent the next morning reviewing every negative experience from my past, asking the Holy Spirit to heal them one by one. I asked Him to heal the pain of being bullied in middle school, losing a close friendship, declaring bankruptcy and many other experiences that needed to be forgiven. After I finished, I felt peaceful, but I wasn't sure anything would come of it. However, I had underestimated the power of healing the past because my life was about to change dramatically.

Only a few days later, HUD unexpectedly accepted the low-ball offer my husband and I had placed on the house. They could have accepted the counteroffer at the higher price, but for some reason, they went with the first lower offer (technically, because we had made a counteroffer, the first contract wasn't valid anymore, but we weren't complaining).

The next day, I received a call from an employer about a graphic design position. What made this call so odd was that I had not applied for the job despite having searched for employment for three years. This employer had found me on social media. Not only did I get the job, but they changed the position to a better title and higher salary.

It was an amazing transformation that I firmly believe resulted from my willingness to forgive my past with the Holy Spirit's help. By healing the negative thoughts and emotions that had acted as blockages between me and the Creative powers, I allowed my natural state of abundance to flow in.

> "The Holy Spirit asks of you but this; bring to Him every secret you have locked away from Him. Open every door to Him, and bid Him enter the darkness and lighten it away. At your request He enters gladly. He brings the light to darkness if you make the darkness open to Him. But what you hide He cannot look upon. He sees for you, and unless you look with Him He cannot see. The vision of Christ is not for Him

alone, but for Him with you. Bring, therefore, all your dark and secret thoughts to Him, and look upon them with Him. He holds the light, and you the darkness. They cannot coexist when both of You together look on them. His judgment must prevail, and He will give it to you as you join your perception to His." T-14.VII.6.1-11

Chapter Questions

Take a moment to reflect on this chapter, and then write down your personal thoughts and insights to the following questions.

1. Consider the significance of asking for healing and guidance from the Holy Spirit, Jesus and divine helpers. How do you incorporate prayer into your own healing journey, and what benefits have you observed from seeking divine assistance?

____

____

____

____

2. Have you ever experienced a shift in your life
    after forgiving past experiences or individuals?
    Share any insights or transformations that
    occurred as a result of this forgiveness process.

____

____

____

____

____

____

____

3. Consider a moment when you felt overwhelmed by fear or grief. How did you cope with these intense emotions, and did you seek support or guidance from spiritual sources?

____

____

____

____

____

4. Have you ever sensed a spiritual presence during difficult times? Describe any moments where you felt supported or guided by a higher power.

____

____

____

____

____

5.   Take a moment to consider how your past
     experiences and emotions relate to your current
     circumstances. What do you need to release?

____

____

____

____

____

____

The next chapter has an exercise that will help you release
what is no longer serving you. This step is *crucial* for
removing the blockages to abundance so please don't skip
the exercise.

Exercise — Releasing the Blockages

"As I walked out the door toward the gate that would lead to my freedom, I knew if I didn't leave my bitterness and hatred behind, I'd still be in prison."

Nelson Mandala

In this exercise, you will actively seek help from the Holy Spirit to heal any negative experiences from your past. These experiences act as blockages that prevent the abundance of the universe from freely entering and enriching your life.

When you **don't** heal your past, you create a future that aligns with your negative thoughts and emotions. To correct this, the best course of action is to let the Holy Spirit heal your past and help you let go of what is no longer serving you. This way, you can fully embrace the present moment with loving thoughts and emotions that manifest a joyful and abundant future.

To begin this exercise, find a place where you won't be disturbed. My favorite place is on my bed with the door closed. Sit comfortably and close your eyes.

Now set the intention to let one of your negative experiences come to the forefront of your mind, such as when you were harassed at school or work or your significant other cheated on you, or the after-effects of an abusive parent, loss of a loved one, a careless remark, etc. You may have to forgive others. You may have to forgive yourself.

When the first negative experience comes to your attention, try to remain emotionally neutral. You do not want to empower it. Observe it briefly to identify what needs to be let go, and then say to the Holy Spirit, **"I release this negative experience to you. I do not want it. Please take it and heal it. Thank you."** Envision the negative experience floating away from you as the Holy Spirit heals it, releasing it from your mind, heart and cosmic blueprint.

Then wait for the next experience to present itself.

If your mind drifts, come back to the present moment and reset your intention to allow a negative experience from your past to come into your awareness for healing.

There is no set time for performing this exercise, but it usually takes much longer the first time.

Occasionally, when you repeat this exercise, you will notice the same negative experience reappearing, which implies that you didn't completely forgive it initially.

This is another opportunity for healing. The effort is always worth it, even if it takes multiple attempts, because eventually, you will be able to forgive the negative experience and all the rest of them.

Healing Your Current Difficulties

In addition to healing the past, you can use the "Releasing the Blockages" exercise when you experience difficulties in the present moment. Whether it's someone cutting you off in traffic or dealing with a difficult situation, you can ask the Holy Spirit to heal the situation and your negative thoughts and emotions, as well as guide you so you can take the best course of action.

You don't have to find a private space to do this. You can silently say a prayer in the midst of the conflict and allow the Holy Spirit's guidance to enter your mind, offering loving suggestions. You might be prompted to leave the situation or discover a level of patience you didn't realize you possessed, or whatever else is appropriate for the circumstance.

If you forget to ask for healing and/or guidance while the situation is occurring, ask as soon as possible. The sooner you ask, the sooner you'll feel better.

You might struggle to forgive someone if you feel they don't deserve it, especially if the abuse or conflict is ongoing. However, bear in mind that people come into your life to teach you what needs to be healed within yourself.

Next is a parable that explains this concept well.

Once, a monk rowed to the middle of a lake to meditate. There he sat with his eyes closed, feeling the sun on his face as he quieted his mind and enjoyed the present moment.

Suddenly, something bumped against his rowboat. The monk's eyes flashed open and he saw another rowboat pressed against his. He became angry that someone could be so careless and was about to shout at them, but the rowboat was empty. It had come untied from the dock.

At that moment, the monk realized his anger already existed within himself. The untethered rowboat had simply been the catalyst that brought his deep-seated anger to the surface of his awareness. The monk understood he needed to heal the anger within himself. It had nothing to do with the empty rowboat.

Don't hesitate to forgive others because when you do so, you are healing yourself. Anyone who brings out negative emotions in you is acting as a catalyst to show you an aspect of yourself that needs to be healed.

Chapter Questions

Take a moment to reflect on the exercise you just performed, and then answer the following questions.

1. What were you able to release during the exercise?

____

____

____

____

____

____

____

2. Have you noticed any recurring negative experiences or emotions in your life? What do you think these patterns might be trying to teach you?

____

____

____

____

____

3. Consider a difficult situation you're currently facing. How do you typically respond to such challenges? Do you think inviting the Holy Spirit's guidance could change your approach?

____

____

____

____

---

4. Think about someone who has caused you pain or frustration. Can you see any way in which their actions or words might reflect something within yourself that needs healing?

Envision the Future as If It is Happening Now

"To bring anything into your life, imagine it's already there." Richard Bach

To manifest the life you desire, you must envision the future as if it is happening now. This is because your thoughts show the Creative powers what you want to manifest. If you envision what you want as if it is somewhere in the distant future, then the Creative powers will create that reality, but always at a distance — like a dangling carrot that you never quite reach.

For example, instead of saying, "I will be rich *one day*," which would cause your wealth to always be somewhere in the future and never today, you should say, "I *am* rich," as if it were true today. If you desire to be healthier, instead of saying, "I need healing," you could say, "I *am* healing," or "I *am* well, strong and vibrant." Sure, it will feel silly at first, but the Creative powers are very literal.

When you take the time to observe your thoughts and words, you will notice how often you project your happiness, health, freedom and abundance to some distant future. When you catch yourself, stop and correct yourself.

> "Thoughts begin in the mind of the thinker, from which they reach outward. This is as true of God's Thinking as it is of yours. Because your mind is split, you can perceive as well as think. Yet perception cannot escape the basic laws of mind. You perceive from your mind and project your perceptions outward. Although perception of any kind is unreal, you made it and the Holy Spirit can therefore use it well. He can inspire perception and lead it toward God. This convergence seems to be far in the future only because your mind is not in perfect alignment with the idea, and therefore does not want it now." T-6.II.9.1-8

By focusing on the present moment without fear of the past or future, you can manifest with an untarnished, focused mind. Your thoughts will be more powerful because of your clarity and fearlessness. Fear constructs a barrier to the abundance of the universe.

> "The Holy Spirit would undo all of this *now*. Fear is not of the present, but only of the past and future, which do not exist. There is no fear in the present when each instant stands clear and separated from the

past, without its shadow reaching out into the future. Each instant is a clean, untarnished birth, in which the Son of God emerges from the past into the present. And the present extends forever. It is so beautiful and so clean and free of guilt that nothing but happiness is there. No darkness is remembered, and immortality and joy are now." T-15.I.8.1-7

I remember a time when I applied "envisioning the future as if it is happening now" to a direct mail campaign I was hired to create. My client was an insurance company specializing in medical malpractice. They aimed to attract doctors with impeccable records, but these doctors were highly sought after by all the insurance companies. This campaign was made even more challenging because it was my client's first attempt to reach this exclusive group. Convincing these doctors to switch to a company without brand recognition would be difficult, especially without the promise of premium savings.

I had two weeks to create the direct mail campaign concept, but as the days passed, I found that every idea I had was uninspired. My fears of being unable to develop a concept had blocked my creativity.

The night before the brochure mockup was due, I lay in bed worrying because I had never missed a deadline. Desperate to save myself, I pleaded to the universe for a dream that would provide me with the perfect concept, and then fell asleep.

During the night, I dreamed of a man sitting at a drafting table, holding a brochure. He showed me the cover design and flipped it open to reveal the inside pages. The brochure design and concept were perfect! The concept compared my client's stellar rating, dedication and quest for excellence with the doctor's perfect track record.

I was excited in the morning and couldn't wait to create the brochure mockup. I almost felt guilty for taking the concept and design suggestions, but I assured myself it wasn't cheating — after all, they had been given to me.

I presented the brochure mockup to the very impressed marketing director that afternoon. However, she had reservations about claiming to be the best choice because of the insurance company's lack of recognition in the top-tier market. I convinced her to act as if they were a key player. If they didn't believe it, who would?

The campaign was very successful despite my ignorance of the principles of manifestation at the time. But that didn't stop the Creative powers from taking effect because we are constantly creating, even when we are not conscious of it.

The campaign was successful because:

- I asked the universe for inspiration and received it.

- Both the marketing director and I had powerful desires for the campaign to succeed. Our thoughts and excitement went into the universe daily as we discussed the best way to launch the campaign.

- The direct mailer presented the insurance company's future vision as a present reality.

To manifest your heart's desires, you need to visualize your manifestations as if they were occurring in the present moment because the present moment is your point of power. When you are focused on the present moment, you are more fully connected to your spirit and the Divine, allowing the abundance of the Creative powers to flow freely into your life.

Don't let your past act like an anchor around your neck, and don't let your worries about the future distract you from the present moment. When you think about the future, think only about what you want to happen, but visualize it as if it is happening now.

Embracing the present allows you to step outside the confines of the Dream, which is always offering you the past because the Dream was dreamed long ago and you are reviewing what has already occurred. The Course teaches us that the ego keeps us trapped in a cycle of replaying past memories and projecting them onto the future, bypassing the present, thus perpetuating a sense of guilt, regret and limitation.

The ego presents a "predetermined" future by using your past experiences, judgments and beliefs to interpret and shape your current reality, often distorting your perception of the present moment. But you don't have to accept the ego's illusions. You can select a better alternative to the Dream.

The Dream is similar to a movie with various alternate scenes. We can choose the scene we want to experience, instead of being stuck with the one that would have played out if we hadn't intervened. Our experiences are a direct result of the choices we make, and we always have the power to make a different choice.

According to the Course, the present moment is where true perception and the experience of peace reside, as it is free from the distortions of past memories and future worries.

As someone who has been practicing shamanic healing for two decades, I have had the opportunity to observe many instances of healing and miracles, both for myself and others. During shamanic journeys, I perceive the outcome as if it has already occurred, even if the transformation takes weeks or months to unfold within our earthly realm of time and space. For successful healing and miracles, it has been necessary to see the outcomes as if they were already true *now*.

Chapter Questions

Take a moment to reflect on this chapter, and then write down your personal thoughts and insights to the following questions.

1. How do past memories and future worries impact your ability to remain present and focused on manifesting your heart's desires?

2. Reflect on the quote by Richard Bach, "To bring anything into your life, imagine it's already there." How does this principle align with your understanding of the manifestation process? Can you recall any specific instances in your life where this principle proved true?

____

____

____

____

____

3. How does maintaining a focused, untarnished mind contribute to your ability to manifest your desires, and what practices do you employ to cultivate mental clarity and alignment with the Creative powers?

____

____

____

____

____

____

4. Have you ever experienced moments of
    inspiration or guidance that seemed to come from
    a higher source or inner knowing? How did
    following these insights impact the outcome?

____

____

____

____

____

____

____

How to Move Forward

"You are always deciding whether to keep things the same or change them. Indecision is a decision to accept things as they are."

How do you discover what you want to experience in life? And once you decide on something, how do you know if it is in your best interest, will make you happy and furthers your special function?

In previous attempts to decide my life's path, I hit the same roadblock over and over again because I couldn't determine if my ideas were in my best interest spiritually, mentally or financially.

I thought I would be able to shamanic journey for the answers, but each time I journeyed, Jesus and my other spirit guides told me, "Follow your heart." I felt the lack of outright answers had to do with honoring my Free Will because if they had told me what to do, I might have felt obligated to do it. But I also felt that my *expectations* of them being unable to answer my questions had prevented them from being able to answer me.

Earlier in this book, I mentioned, "The question limits the answer." Here is the verse from the URtext again: "Choose your questions wisely, meaning the more limits imposed in your question, the more limited your response from the Creative powers will be." After reading the verse, it occurred to me that my expectations and beliefs had limited the divine helpers' abilities to guide me. I needed to allow them to help me with all matters in life, not just spiritual or healing concerns.

> "It is only because you think that you can run some little part, or deal with certain aspects of your life alone, that the guidance of the Holy Spirit is limited. Thus would you make Him undependable, and use this fancied undependability as an excuse for keeping certain dark lessons from Him. And by so limiting the guidance that you would accept, you are unable to depend on miracles to answer all your problems for you." T-14.XI.8.4-6

Before, I thought it was my responsibility to manage the smaller aspects of life without seeking help. But now I know the Holy Spirit, Jesus and divine helpers want us to ask for guidance on all matters in our lives because it saves us valuable time and helps us avoid mistakes, enabling us to focus on the more important aspects of our lives.

Because of our inability to foresee the future or fully comprehend the present, any decision we make is inherently flawed, no matter how logical it may seem. When we depend solely on ourselves and neglect to ask for divine guidance, we often make regrettable decisions based on half-truths.

Many years ago, I was sitting next to my grandfather at the family Christmas party. I glanced at him, noticing his striking profile and strong nose. I had often thought he had a Native American appearance, but he identified as Hispanic, just like everyone else on my father's side. Sure, there were signs this wasn't entirely true, such as my second cousin's long black hair that hung down to his waist, but when you're told your entire life you are Hispanic, you assume it's true.

During that period, I collaborated with a law college to promote their Indigenous Law program. The marketing director and I met with an Indigenous assistant professor who was the program's founding director. At the meeting, he educated us on some of the tribe's culture that could influence how the potential students responded to the marketing materials.

Because Native American culture was on my mind, I decided to ask my grandfather, "Are you part Native American?" I felt his energy tighten.

Staring straight ahead, he answered, "Yes," and then stood up, moving away from me to sit beside other relatives.

My grandfather's response differed greatly from mine. I was happy with the news. I had always wanted to be Native American because I loved their reverence for the earth and animals. I'm not exactly sure what my grandfather felt, but it was obvious he didn't like the question.

I walked over to my father and asked him for confirmation, "Are we part Native American?"

"Yes. Your great-grandfather was a full-blooded Apache."

"Why didn't you tell me?"

"You never asked."

Getting answers in my family was never a simple task. But this time, my typically reserved father opened up and shared the stories of how my great-grandfather had crossed paths with Pancho Villa, and smuggled sugar and flour from Mexico into Texas while the Texas Rangers shot at him. When I asked how my great-grandfather reacted to being shot at, my father curtly replied as if the answer was obvious, "He shot back."

After hearing these insights into our family history, I came to the realization that my grandfather may have hidden his heritage because his father was born a few years after Chief Geronimo and the Apache tribes were imprisoned by the U.S. government and held captive in forts or open-air prisons (reservations). Although this is considered a part of ancient history today, I still have vivid memories of my great-grandfather, who passed away when I was five years old.

In addition, after discovering the truth about my ancestry, I better understood my affinity for Native American culture and shamanic journeying.

You and I don't always know if there are skeletons in the family closet or what the future holds. Life continually presents us with half-truths, which is why divine guidance is invaluable. It will lead us in the right direction. Like when I was inspired to enroll in the "Learn About Shamanism" workshop, which I mistakenly believed was a lecture series, but instead, I was taught how to shamanic journey — a practice I never thought I would engage in. Yet, because of all the miracles I witnessed through shamanic journeying, the practice brought me back to a belief in God. The Divine had a perfect understanding of how to work with me — and can do the same for you on your unique path.

Keep an Open Mind

When we have a preconceived notion of the answer, we limit the potential for the Divine to provide additional insights, suggest alternatives or offer corrections to our ideas. To navigate through life's uncertainties, it is crucial that we keep our minds open and trust that the Divine is fully aware of all the possibilities and always looking out for our best interests.

> "When you have learned how to decide with God, all decisions become as easy and as right as breathing. There is no effort, and you will be led as gently as if you were being carried down a quiet path in summer. Only your own volition seems to make deciding hard. The Holy Spirit will not delay in answering your every question what to do. He knows. And He will tell you, and then do it for you." T-14.IV.6.1-6

By being open to the inspiration and opportunities that come our way, we create the possibility of being guided towards a different and potentially better direction than what we could have envisioned for ourselves.

Don't Force It

As a graphic designer, I found the best way to create an inspired design was to review the details of the job, and then let the information ferment in the back of my mind for several days. When I felt a flutter of excitement while thinking about the project, I knew it was time to begin. This practice allowed me to create designs that were better than if I forced the ideas to come. It also saved me valuable time.

Back then, I didn't realize I was manifesting designs by repeatedly thinking about what I wanted and patiently waiting for the universe to send me ideas.

To compensate for tight deadlines that didn't allow me days to ferment on the ideas, I used a technique that allowed me to reach a superconscious state (keep in mind, I didn't know why this process worked at the time; I just knew it did). To perform the technique, I would lie down and let my mind gradually descend into a state between wakefulness and slumber, and then I asked the universe to show me a design. This technique was a delicate balance between not falling asleep and staying alert enough to see what was being presented to me. These designs were my favorites — except for the ones that came to me in my dreams.

In the next chapter, I share an exercise I developed for receiving ideas you can use that is easier than trying to obtain a superconscious state.

The Need to Let Go

In hindsight, it's easy to see how the ending of my graphic design business was a part of my spiritual growth. While working, I kept having intrusive visions of a brick wall. Deep down, I knew it would end. But the money was substantial and I enjoyed being a graphic designer, so I was not willing to give it up without it being pried out of my hands. Yet somehow, I also knew on a spiritual level that I had agreed to its ending.

As the following verse points out, "…the plan will sometimes call for changes in what seem to be external circumstances." When I lost my business, it felt like a rug had been pulled out from under me because I did not know how to move forward, but letting go of my business was necessary to uncover what I truly desired.

> "First, they must go through what might be called 'a period of undoing.' This need not be painful, but it usually is so experienced. It seems as if things are being taken away, and it is rarely understood initially that their lack of value is merely being recognized. How can lack of value be perceived unless the perceiver is in a position where he must see things in a different light? He is not yet at a point at which he can make the shift entirely internally. And so the plan will sometimes call for changes in what seem to be external circumstances. These changes are always helpful."
> M-4.I.A.3.1-7

I tried to reestablish my graphic design business several times, but with little success. I resisted letting go of it because it had served me well for so many years.

But my path had evolved. Eventually, I felt open to new possibilities and a willingness to be guided. I recognized that parting ways with my company was necessary to forge a new path.

We need to let go of what no longer serves us. Part of the process might seem painful, but the more open we are to being guided, the easier it will be to travel on our new path. The Course says we can learn joyfully. It's our resistance that makes it painful.

The ego wants us to cling to our past experiences, especially our mistakes. Let the Holy Spirit heal your past and help you let go of what is no longer serving you so you can fully embrace the present moment and look forward to your future.

> "The ego invests heavily in the past, and in the end believes that the past is the only aspect of time that is meaningful. Remember that its emphasis on guilt enables it to ensure its continuity by making the future like the past, and thus avoiding the present. By the notion of paying for the past in the future, the past becomes the determiner of the future, making them continuous without an intervening present."
> T-13.IV.4.2-4

What If You Don't Know What You Want?

Having clear goals is crucial because they ensure that your life unfolds in accordance with your true desires.

When it comes to discovering what you want, you'll be amazed by the remarkable power of starting with a simple request for guidance. For example, you could say to the Holy Spirit, "Please help me know what I want." It's short and sweet. The answer doesn't always come immediately, but it does come eventually.

> "The ego cannot oppose the laws of God any more than you can, but it can interpret them according to what it wants, just as you can. That is why the question, "What do you want?" must be answered. You are answering it every minute and every second, and each moment of decision is a judgment that is anything but ineffectual. Its effects will follow automatically until the decision is changed." T-5.V.6.1-4

At times, your ability to receive divine guidance can be blocked by your busy mind. In that case, I recommend you do the exercise in the next chapter. It will help you focus your attention and establish a connection with your higher self, which is connected to the all-knowing divine power, to receive new ideas.

Chapter Questions

Take a moment to reflect on this chapter, and then write down your personal thoughts and insights to the following questions.

1. Contemplate on the concept that "Indecision is a decision to accept things as they are." How does this idea resonate with your own experiences of decision-making? Have there been instances where indecision has led to accepting a situation you later wished to change?

---

2. Consider the idea of preconceived notions limiting your ability to receive guidance. How do your own expectations and beliefs shape the guidance you seek or receive? Are there areas of your life where you could benefit from letting go of preconceived ideas and remaining open to new insights?

____

____

____

____

____

3. Reflect on the importance of asking for guidance in all aspects of life, not just spiritual or healing concerns. How might seeking divine guidance on everyday matters contribute to better outcomes in your life?

____

____

____

____

____

____

4. Reflect on the concept of letting go of what no longer serves you. How do you discern when it's time to release something from your life? What practices or strategies can you use to facilitate the process of letting go?

____

____

____

____

____

____

5. Reflect on the power of clear goals in shaping the direction of your life. Do you have any goals in mind? If yes, list them below.

Exercise — Discovering What You Want

"When you make contact with your Higher Self, you'll have the support of Nature, which will allow for the manifestation of all you desire." Deepak Chopra

This exercise will help you connect with your higher self to receive ideas and inspiration that will benefit your life. When working with your higher self, there isn't the limitation of "honoring the free will" since you and your higher self are one and the same.

Your imagination is a powerful tool because it comes from your higher self, which has access to all the possibilities held within the universe. Think of these possibilities as parallel universes that are waiting to be claimed.

You have multiple options to choose from within the universe. The Course says you do not have infinite choices because that would delay your awakening indefinitely, but you have more than enough choices to satisfy your desires. These choices are part of the original ancient Dream, but they have been obscured by your fears, doubts and guilt, which stem from the ego's belief in separation from God.

You can select an ancient "new" idea to enter your life through your intention and focused thought and the Holy Spirit's help in leading you toward truth. Imagine your choices as a library where you can select any book you want and return it when you are done with it. Another way to think about this is to imagine yourself as a video game character striving to reach the next level. The level already exists, but it remains only as a possibility until you reach it.

> "The ancient new ideas they bring will be the happy consequences of a Cause so ancient that It far exceeds the span of memory which your perception sees." T-28.I.7.9

> "What happened long ago seems to be happening now. Choices made long since appear to be open; yet to be made. What has been learned and understood and long ago passed by is looked upon as a new thought, a fresh idea, a different approach. Because your will is free you can accept what has already happened at any time you choose, and only then will you realize that it was always there." M-2.3.2-5

To begin this exercise, say, "I want to know what I want."

Now, close your eyes and envision a white mist rolling over you. Walk through the white mist, knowing you are safe. Your steps are slow and steady. The answers you seek will be on the other side.

When you finally walk out of the white mist, you enter a darkened, empty movie theater with only one seat. You sit down.

The movie screen is covered by a red velvet curtain. You pull a lever beside your seat and the curtain opens to reveal a blank screen.

Your higher self, unseen in the projector room, selects a movie from a large rack filled with numerous movies. The big screen flickers and the movie begins to play, providing you with ideas and inspiration. If you don't like the movie, push the lever to close the curtain, and then pull the lever to re-open the curtain. A new movie will begin to play. Once you like what you see, immerse yourself in the movie. Observe the sights, sounds and emotions evoked in you.

Parts of the movie might seem disjointed, fuzzy or strange, like a dream. That is okay. What is being presented to you are pieces of a puzzle that will come together soon enough. For now, stay open to all of it, even when it makes little sense.

You can repeat opening and closing the curtain as many times as you want. Each movie will provide its own set of ideas and inspiration.

Once you are done watching the movies, close the curtain, and then stand up and walk up the aisle towards the white mist billowing out of the doorway. Step through the white mist to return to this reality.

Chapter Questions

Take a moment to reflect on the exercise you just performed, and then answer the following questions.

1. What ideas and suggestions did you receive?

____

____

____

____

____

____

____

2. Describe who or what you saw, felt, sensed and heard.

____

____

____

____

____

3. Was what you saw literal or symbolic?

____

____

____

____

4. What was the oddest thing about what you saw?

____

____

____

____

____

5. What parts felt true?

____

____

____

____

6. Did you sense something that wasn't readily apparent?

____

____

____

____

Next, review your answers to these chapter questions and transfer the key points to a list that you can review before bedtime (or at your preferred time).

Moving forward, review your list every day. When you have a new idea, add it to your list. When something no longer feels right, cross it off the list. At this point, don't worry about the details or how you'll make it happen.

Repeat this exercise regularly until you have a crystal-clear vision of what you want to manifest in your life. You may see distinct possibilities each time you do this exercise, or you may see the same possibility returning, but with added details.

After you decide what you want to manifest, spend 10-15 minutes _every day_ visualizing your ideas as if they were true now. In this way, you are attracting the universe's options toward you.

Watch Out for the Speed Bumps

"If you realized how powerful your thoughts are, you would never think a negative thought." Peace Pilgrim

This chapter focuses on some of the reasons people don't experience the results they desire when applying the fundamentals of the Miraculous Life Process.

Hard Work Can't Outweigh Your Thoughts

Most people believe they must work hard to get what they want and they *will* have to work hard because the Creative powers will honor their belief. But these people will soon grow weary, feeling the rewards aren't a fair exchange for their efforts.

To fully benefit from the Miraculous Life Process, you must give up the belief that you can force things to happen or that with enough hard work, you'll make it to the top. You don't have to pay your dues (to whom?) or need a degree (hire the expertise you need or become self-taught). Your dreams can and will come true once you release the belief that actions are more powerful than thoughts. It's the other way around. Your persistent and heartfelt thoughts cause the universe to align with your desires.

You can work your fingers to the bone, but you can't outwork your negative thoughts. Think of all the people who never get ahead. Something always sabotages their efforts. Until they learn to think positively and align their beliefs and actions with their thoughts, they will continue to receive undesirable results.

Patience is a Virtue

Sometimes, we try to force things to happen instead of waiting for life to unfold in its own time to our desires.

Let me give you an example of an ordinary purchase I intended to make. I went shopping for a reclining sofa and loveseat, but none of the styles seemed "right" — they were either too expensive or didn't match our decor. So instead of buying new furniture, I decided to purchase a padded ottoman we could rest our feet on. I spent hours browsing online, but once again, I ran into a problem because our current furniture was oversized and every ottoman was too small — so I waited to let the universe align with my desires.

A few days later, I had a passing thought about browsing a specific online marketplace. There, I found the perfect ottoman that someone had posted the night before. It was the right size, inexpensive and matched our furniture perfectly. If I had looked earlier, I wouldn't have found it. If I had looked later, it might have been sold. But because I followed my inner guidance and was patient, I got just what I wanted.

When we have a desire, it can take the Creative powers a little while to change the dynamics within this Dream to meet our requests.

> "Those who are certain of the outcome can afford to wait, and wait without anxiety." M-4.VIII.1.1

Watch Out for Negative Thoughts

It is important for you to focus on what you want instead of what you don't want because the Creative powers will give you what you are thinking about. If you are thinking, *I don't have enough money,* then you will continue to not have enough money.

To erase the impact of your negative thoughts, you must first catch yourself thinking about them. When you do, immediately refocus on what you want. Take the time to think positively with all your heart. (Sometimes I say a prayer to heal any possible negative effects from my previous negative thoughts.)

By watching out for negative thoughts, you'll notice how often you have them, and then you will understand why your life isn't quite the way you want it to be.

When any thought enters your mind, it is up to you to decide whether to accept it or reject it. Regardless of whether the thought is negative or positive, your belief in its reality and time spent focusing on it may cause it to alter your life. I say "may" because the level of your focus, emotions, consistency and actions all contribute to the outcome.

Lack of Goals

The Course states the importance of knowing what you want in order to achieve positive outcomes. When you have a definite goal in mind, you won't let the obstacles stop you, and you will see the opportunities you may have otherwise missed.

> "Without a clear-cut, positive goal, set at the outset, the situation just seems to happen, and makes no sense until it has already happened. Then you look back at it, and try to piece together what it must have meant. And you will be wrong. Not only is your judgment in the past, but you have no idea what should happen." T-17.VI.3.1-4

> "The value of deciding in advance what you want to happen is simply that you will perceive the situation as a means to *make* it happen. You will therefore make every effort to overlook what interferes with the accomplishment of your objective, and concentrate on everything that helps you meet it." T-17.VI.4.1-2

Your Actions Should Align with Your Spirit

When your actions are aligned with your spirit:

- Your thoughts are pleasant

- Your actions are easy to carry out

- The outcomes are pleasing

You were meant to prosper by doing what you love. Even if what you want to do seems like hard work to others, carrying it out will be easy and fulfilling for you. You'll look forward to getting up in the morning and interacting with the world to express your creativity and desires.

Lack of Clarity

The clearer your mind, the more powerful your thoughts. Be aware of when the ego is using fear-based thoughts to create confusion and distractions in your mind. By staying focused on what you want and following the Holy Spirit's guidance, you will overcome the ego's intrusive thoughts.

Be Trusting

Trust that God established universal laws to ensure you would not be trapped forever within this Dream as a powerless victim and that you would have choices about what you experience in this world.

You possess the power bestowed upon you by God to manifest your own reality, but because your mind is split, you need help making decisions. You can count on the Holy Spirit, Jesus and divine helpers to lead you to a rewarding life.

> "The teachers of God have trust in the world, because they have learned it is not governed by the laws the world made up. It is governed by a power that is *in* them but not *of* them. It is this power that keeps all things safe." M-4.I.1.4-6

> "When this power has once been experienced, it is impossible to trust one's own petty strength again. Who would attempt to fly with the tiny wings of a sparrow when the mighty power of an eagle has been given him? And who would place his faith in the shabby offerings of the ego when the gifts of God are laid before him?" M-4.I.2.1-3

Be Generous

The universe reflects your state of mind so when you are in a generous state, the universe is generous to you.

Consider the attributes you desire from other people: gratitude, fairness, recognition, inclusion, support, love, etc. These are the same things you should give them because what you give is what you'll likely get back. However, the act of giving should not be done solely to receive something in return. It is also about recognizing God in everyone you meet because when you see God in others, you also find God in yourself.

> "Believe in your brothers because I believe in you, and you will learn that my belief in you is justified. Believe

in me *by* believing in them, for the sake of what God gave them. They will answer you if you learn to ask only truth of them. Do not ask for blessings without blessing them, for only in this way can you learn how blessed you are. By following this way you are seeking the truth in you." T-9.II.8.1-5

Be Tolerant

Cultivate a mindset that respects other people's choices, even when they are different from your own. Everyone must find their own way in life. Giving others the freedom to be themselves allows you to follow your heart without self-condemnation.

"It is not up to you to change your brother, but merely to accept him as he is. His errors do not come from the truth that is in him, and only this truth is yours. His errors cannot change this, and can have no effect at all on the truth in you. To perceive errors in anyone, and to react to them as if they were real, is to make them real to you. You will not escape paying the price for this, not because you are being punished for it, but because you are following the wrong guide and will therefore lose your way." T-9.III.6.4-8

Conflicting Wishes

If a person has two conflicting wishes, then obviously one of them will not work out.

"Fear is always a sign of strain, arising whenever what you want conflicts with what you do. This situation arises in two ways: First, you can choose to do conflicting things, either simultaneously or successively. This produces conflicted behavior, which is intolerable to you because the part of the mind that wants to do something else is outraged. Second, you can behave as you think you should, but without entirely wanting to do so. This produces consistent behavior, but entails great strain. In both cases, the mind and the behavior are out of accord, resulting in a situation in which you are doing what you do not wholly want to do. This arouses a sense of coercion that usually produces rage, and projection is likely to follow. Whenever there is fear, it is because you have not made up your mind. Your mind is therefore split, and your behavior inevitably becomes erratic." T-2.VI.5.1-9

Don't Let Fear Get in the Way

The Course says the core reason we are afraid of change is because our first experience with change was our separation from heaven (even if the separation only happened in our mind). With this underlying fear, it's difficult to move forward because we are afraid our decision will lead to a mistake that pulls us even further away from heaven. Being aware of this unconscious fear can help us understand when it is preventing us from doing something that feels right for us.

"Change is always fearful to the separated, because they cannot conceive of it as a move towards healing the separation. They always perceive it as a move toward further separation, because the separation was their first experience of change." T-4.I.2.2-3

Another reason people can become afraid is when they experience a transformation that cannot be explained by the laws of science or the accepted principles of the world; they have to acknowledge there is a greater force outside of their reality. The results of their manifestation might challenge their beliefs and lead to fear.

"The Holy Spirit is invisible, but you can see the results of His Presence, and through them you will learn that He is there. What He enables you to do is clearly not of this world, for miracles violate every law of reality as this world judges it." T-12.VII.3.1-2

Fear is capable of canceling your manifestation request because it is telling the Creative powers you don't really want what you are saying you want. On one hand, you are shouting, "I want this," while on the other, you are simultaneously shouting, "I am afraid of what I want." You have created conflicting requests and fear usually wins.

"Let us suppose, then, that what you ask of the Holy Spirit is what you really want, but you are still afraid of it. Should this be the case, your attainment of it would no longer *be* what you want." T-9.II.2.1-2

Prayer won't conquer your fear because the Holy Spirit will never force anything upon you, even something as wonderful as abundance or health. To break through the problem of fear hindering your requests, ask the Holy Spirit to heal whatever is causing your fear so you can move forward and get what you desire. You can say something as simple as, "I'm afraid. Please heal the cause of my fear," and then release the outcome to the Holy Spirit.

Fear shows you are relying solely on yourself.

> "Whenever you are afraid, it is a sure sign that you have allowed your mind to miscreate and have not allowed me to guide it." T-2.VI.2.10

Make Sure You Truly Want It

Asking for things that either don't serve you or you don't really want can be a reason you don't get them — your thoughts are misaligned with your heart's desires. For instance, if the only reason you want a bigger house is because your sibling has one, then you don't truly desire it (or the large mortgage that goes with it). It takes courage to say "no" to what doesn't feel right for you.

You need to make sure that what you are asking for is what *you* truly want. Doing soul searching and asking for guidance is important, but so is following your heart and not giving in to societal pressures.

Allow Change to Occur

Think of all the wonderful changes in your life that were stressful — even if you desired them:

- Getting married

- Moving into your first house or apartment

- Having a baby

- Being promoted

If you want something different, something has to change. Pay attention to your resistance. When are you procrastinating? Why aren't you following through on your inspiration? When are you letting your doubts and fears take precedence in your mind?

Be honest with yourself. If the changes are too much for you, scale back your plans. Take baby steps. You will know if your plans are good for you by how you feel when making them.

Your decisions and actions should feel good. That doesn't mean there won't be butterflies in your stomach when you try something new. Feel the adrenaline coursing through your veins. You're alive! Enjoy the ride.

Resisting Help

The Holy Spirit, Jesus and divine helpers are always speaking to us, but we often don't hear them because our minds are filled with miscellaneous thoughts that drown out their quiet voices.

Why do we let these thoughts parade through our mind? Because we enjoy creating with our thoughts, even if things aren't turning out quite like we hoped. We're like first-graders drawing with crayons, and even though our drawings are rudimentary, we don't want anyone else touching them or offering suggestions. However, if we accepted the Divine's suggestions, our drawings would turn into amazing masterpieces. But honestly, we are usually more concerned about maintaining control rather than the quality of our drawings.

> "It is possible to reach a state in which you bring your mind under my guidance without conscious effort, but this implies a willingness that you have not developed as yet. The Holy Spirit cannot ask more than you are willing to do. The strength to do comes from your undivided decision." T-2.VI.6.1-3

Feeling Unworthy

Success has nothing to do with being worthy. Even ruthless business people have achieved great wealth because they spent a great deal of time focusing on what they wanted. You don't have to justify why you deserve to be successful, because everyone deserves success. There is nothing you can do to make yourself worthy or holy because you already are.

"Your worth is not established by teaching or learning. Your worth is established by God."
T-4.I.7.1-2

The Ego's Sabotage

The manifestation process would be easier if your ego wasn't busy trying to override your efforts. Your ego will tell you that you are not worthy or that God has forsaken you because it wants you to believe you're a powerless victim of life. However, once you learn how to change your life through manifestation and miracles, you can let go of your fears and embrace your divine power.

When Things Don't Go Your Way

When you encounter situations where things don't go your way, you may start doubting the Miraculous Life Process. You may wonder if things will ever go your way or if the process is a waste of time. When you reach this point, remember that you are still building your inner strength and mental fortitude, which means your foundation is weak. But it will become stronger through persistence and divine assistance.

Be Careful Who You Share Your Dreams With

Nothing drains the power from your manifestation process faster than the doubts and fears of friends, family and colleagues. Be careful who you share your dreams with. Even if they mean well and believe they are looking out for your best interests, their discouraging words can infiltrate your thoughts, raising your own doubts and significantly slowing the manifestation process. Only share your plans with trusted allies who you can count on to support you.

Chapter Questions

Take a moment to reflect on this chapter, and then write down your personal thoughts and insights to the following questions.

1. Think back on a time when you believed that hard work alone could bring you success. Did this belief yield the desired results? Why or why not?

____

____

____

____

____

2. Can you recall a situation where patience played a crucial role in achieving your desired outcome? How did waiting for the right moment influence the result?

____

____

____

____

3. Think about a time when you effortlessly and joyfully took action. How did being in alignment with your spirit affect the outcome of your efforts?

____

____

____

____

____

4. Trust is often emphasized as essential in spiritual growth. Reflect on your level of trust in the Holy Spirit, Jesus and divine helpers. How does trust (or lack thereof) impact your ability to manifest?

____

____

____

____

5. Reflect on a time when you struggled to accept someone else's choices or beliefs. How did your lack of tolerance affect your relationship with that person?

____

____

____

____

____

6. Have you ever found yourself torn between conflicting wishes and fear? How did you resolve this internal conflict?

____

____

____

____

____

7. Consider whether you've ever asked for something you didn't truly want or need. What motivated this request, and what were the consequences?

____

____

____

____

---

8. Reflect on a significant change in your life. How did your resistance or acceptance of change influence the outcome?

---

9. Reflect on a time when you felt unworthy of success or happiness. How did this feeling impact your ability to embrace either of them?

---

10. Reflect on a recent setback or disappointment. How did you respond to this situation, and what did you learn from it?

You Are Powerful Beyond Measure

"Our deepest fear is not that we are inadequate. Our deepest fear is that we are powerful beyond measure. It is our light, not our darkness that most frightens us. We ask ourselves, 'Who am I to be brilliant, gorgeous, talented, fabulous?' Actually, who are you not to be?" Marianne Williamson

We have all the power of our Creator. We have never lost this power — we have only forgotten it.

Most likely, the hardest thing for you to believe when practicing the fundamentals of the Miraculous Life Process will be that *you* have the power to create a life filled with happiness, health and abundance. Each time you think, "It won't work for me because...," remember, you have access to the unlimited power that comes from God.

> "Power and glory belong to God alone. So do you. God gives whatever belongs to Him because He gives of Himself, and everything belongs to Him. Giving of yourself is the function He gave you. Fulfilling it perfectly will let you remember what you *have* of Him, and by this you will remember also what you *are* in Him. You cannot be powerless to do this, because this is your power." T-8.III.8.1-6

Each day, take the time to envision the dream life you want as if it were happening now. The more you think about your dream life, the more power you give to your thoughts. And as you believe in your dreams, you will develop strong emotions that add additional power to your thoughts — speeding up the process considerably. Plus, because your ideas are at the forefront of your mind, you will more easily recognize opportunities when they arrive.

If you think you can't change your life, keep Robert Smalls in mind. Smalls was born a slave in 1839 in South Carolina. He was a defiant man who frequently found himself in the Beaufort jail. During the Civil War, his master rented him out to the city of Charleston, and Smalls became one of the best pilots in the area, navigating the winding channels in and out of the harbor to avoid the Union patrols. He kept his eyes open for any opportunity that might allow him to escape. It finally came when a new captain arrived. The captain and his crew often left the ship unattended at night to spend time with their families. Smalls planned to seize the ship with the help of the enslaved crew. Undertaking such a dangerous task, they would face certain death if they were caught.

On the night of May 13, 1862, Smalls seized the ship, backtracking to pick up his family and other slaves, blowing the ship's horn when passing Confederate forts and batteries, and flashing the correct Navy signals. He wore the captain's coat and signature straw hat, and even folded his arms like the captain, passing for white in the early morning light. When he neared a Union blockade, he replaced the Rebel flags with a white bed sheet to prevent being fired upon. His ship safely reached the shore. Smalls freed himself, his family and the other slaves, totaling 16 people.

During the war, Smalls earned a promotion to the rank of captain and was recognized as one of the highest-paid black soldiers.

When President Lincoln invited Smalls to the White House, he asked him why he had attempted such a dangerous mission. Smalls simply replied, "Freedom."

As a reward for stealing a ship from the Confederate army, Smalls received $1,500. With it, he purchased his former master's house in Beaufort and started a general store, a school for black children and a newspaper. He also got elected to the U.S. House of Representatives for five non-consecutive terms.

Smalls followed the principles of manifestation. He first decided that he wanted freedom and stayed focused on that desire, which prompted the universe to provide him with the opportunities to learn the skills and have the experiences necessary for him to later create his daring plan. When the time was right, Smalls acted on the opportunity to steal that ship despite the dangers. Smalls, a former slave, succeeded in life. Surely, you can achieve your heart's desires, too.

Jane Goodall is another success story. She is an English primatologist and anthropologist who is considered the world's foremost expert on wild chimpanzees. Did you know that when she started studying chimpanzees, she had no college degree? It was only after she was fully engaged in her research that she attended Cambridge University and then went to Newnham College to get a PhD degree in ethology.

Her love of chimpanzees brought her to Kenya as a young woman. She found work as a secretary, then made an appointment to discuss animals with the prominent Kenyan archaeologist and paleontologist Louis Leakey. Goodall began working for him as a secretary, but soon was sent to Gombe Stream National Park to study primate behavior with two other behaviorists. Her mother had to accompany her to satisfy the chief warden's concerns for her safety.

Goodall's findings revolutionized the understanding of chimpanzees when she observed many behavioral similarities between them and humans, such as hugging, kissing and even tickling. The primates used tools, such as sticks to fish for termites within their mounds. Goodall has worked diligently on conservation and animal welfare issues and was named a UN Messenger of Peace in 2002.

Goodall didn't wait to get her degree to follow her dreams. She followed her heart to Kenya. Her passion opened doors for her. Her clear focus made her dreams come true. And as each event unfurled, it created more opportunities for her, which she gladly took. She could have waited to get her degree first, but wisely followed her heart. Things needed to play out in the time frame, just as they did. If she had used her practical mind to decide, her life would have turned out very differently.

Don't wait for things to be perfect for you to act. Your desire will create opportunities, and if you seize them, they will alter your life in amazing ways. Just imagine if Jane Goodall had gone the typical route of attending college first so she could feel qualified to study chimpanzees. Or if Robert Smalls had let his fears stop him from stealing the ship he steered towards his freedom. Instead, they followed their hearts to live remarkable lives.

Too often, we don't dream big enough because we believe smaller goals are more obtainable. If you are holding yourself back from a life-changing achievement, take the time to recognize the fear that is keeping you from dreaming bigger. Are you holding onto past failures? Is it because you've never achieved greatness before and don't think it's possible? Are you afraid of people doubting you? Are you afraid of losing your family savings? Take the time to sit quietly and observe your thoughts to discover your concerns.

Your greatness was written in the stars. It's up to you to claim it and act on it.

Chapter Questions

Take a moment to reflect on this chapter, and then write down your personal thoughts and insights to the following questions.

1. Reflect on a time when you felt hesitant to embrace your own power and potential. What fears or doubts held you back from fully acknowledging your capabilities?

____

____

____

____

____

2. Reflect on the story of Robert Smalls and his daring escape to freedom and Jane Goodall's pursuit of her passion for studying chimpanzees. What lessons or inspiration can you draw from

their experiences about the power of determination and belief in one's dreams?

____

____

____

____

____

3. Think about a goal or heartfelt desire you've been hesitant to pursue because of fear or self-doubt. What specific fears or concerns have been holding you back from taking action?

____

____

____

____

____

4. This chapter's message encourages us not to wait for perfect conditions to pursue our dreams. How does this idea resonate with you? Have you ever waited for the "right time" to act, and then regretted missing an opportunity?

____

____

____

____

5. Consider the idea that your greatness is already within you, waiting to be claimed and acted upon. Can you list your characteristics, abilities and achievements that you are proud of?

____

____

____

____

____

Exercise — The Secret to Miraculous Results

"And, when you want something, all the universe conspires in helping you to achieve it." Paulo Coelho,

The Alchemist

All thoughts contain power. And when combined with strong emotions, thoughts become even more powerful. If you were to think about what you want with strong emotions every day, it would alter your life. But if you wish to boost your creations to a miraculous level, I urge you to do the exercise in this chapter.

One thing that surprised me when I first read *A Course in Miracles* was how it aligned with the concepts of shamanism. Through shamanic journeying, I've been able to receive healing and guidance by working with spirit guides (Jesus Christ is one of my spirit guides).

These divine interactions have led to faster and more amazing results (and sometimes outright miracles) more often than when I used only my thoughts and emotions. I believe the results were more immediate and dramatic because my spirit was connected to the divine power in a pure state, cutting through the blockages of my mind and allowing the divine energy to flow freely.

When I shamanic journey, it is crucial that I ask my spirit guides for their help in order for the healing to be accomplished. Here is one of my favorite verses from *A Course in Miracles* that explains why the task of asking is so important: "The miracle extends without your help, but **you are needed that it can begin**. Accept the miracle of healing, and it will go forth because of what it is. It is its nature to extend itself the instant it is born." We have to ask the Holy Spirit, Jesus and divine helpers for miracles in order to receive them, except in rare instances of divine intervention. In addition, our miracles will have a ripple effect throughout the universe, positively affecting many others.

> "This world is full of miracles. They stand in shining silence next to every dream of pain and suffering, of sin and guilt. They are the dream's alternative, the choice to be the dreamer, rather than deny the active role in making up the dream." T-28.II.12.1-3

You don't need to know how to shamanic journey to receive miraculous results because connecting to the divine power can be done in many ways, such as prayer. Think of this exercise as a focused two-way prayer in which you establish a strong connection to the divine power to amplify your desires and receive guidance and miracles.

To begin this exercise, find a quiet, comfortable place to sit or lie down where no one will disturb you.

Take three deep breaths to bring yourself into the present moment.

Now, close your eyes and envision a white mist rolling over you. Walk through the white mist, knowing you are safe. Your steps are slow and steady. Eventually, you come to the other side of the white mist and step out onto solid ground.

There is a tunnel entrance in front of you, burrowed in a hillside, but the tunnel is long and dark, and you prefer not to enter it. So you decide to sidestep the tunnel by walking to the left of it. (By refusing to enter the tunnel, you are reminding yourself that you always have a choice about what you want to experience in life. The tunnel can represent your fears, the demands of the world, etc.)

You climb up the hill and reach a grassy bluff. From this summit, you can see the lush valley below and misty mountains in the background. Your divine helper, who has been waiting to meet you, is sitting there. (They could be anyone because the Divine can take any form. Your divine helper could be Jesus, a spirit guide, an animal, an angel, Buddha, a guru, an ancestor, etc.)

"Are other teachers possible, to lead the way to those who speak in different tongues and appeal to different symbols? Certainly there are. Would God leave anyone without a very present help in time of trouble; a savior who can symbolize Himself? Yet do we need a many-faceted curriculum, not because of content differences, but because symbols must shift and change to suit the need. Jesus has come to answer yours. In him you find God's Answer." M-23.7.2-7

"Is he God's only Helper? No, indeed. For Christ takes many forms with different names until their oneness can be recognized. But Jesus is for you the bearer of Christ's single message of the Love of God. You need no other." C-5.6.1-5

Sit beside your divine helper. Explain to them what you want to manifest and ask them for their advice so you can feel confident before making your request.

Once you are ready, silently shout out your request into the blue sky, letting it soar into the universe to be answered.

Keep in mind that the way you word your request can limit the response. For instance, instead of shouting, "I want to make $300,000 a year," you could shout, "I *am* making $300,000 a year *or more*." This way, you remove the cap (limitation) to your request, and state it as if it was already true. Perhaps you already have some ideas on how to earn the amount of money you desire, but if you don't, you can consult with your divine helper, or ask your higher self to send you ideas by using the "Discovering What You Want" exercise.

If you want to heal a physical ailment, such as high blood sugar levels, you could silently shout, "I *am* healthy. My blood sugar *is* normal." But you would also have to follow the guidance to eat healthy and exercise regularly.

Keep all your requests in the present tense as if they were already a part of your life to prevent projecting them into the distant future.

Be open to alternative opportunities, as your desires may not be fulfilled exactly as you expect, and they may take longer to come into your life than you want, but keep in mind that the Holy Spirit will only alter events in a way where everyone involved benefits. This means sometimes you will have to wait for things to fall into place. If you requested a specific job position, you might not get it, but your desire has gone out into the universe, so expect a job position that is a better fit for you than the one you didn't get. "Better" is a subjective word. It might mean the job has a shorter commute so you can spend more time at home. It might mean you get a job with lower pay, but you learn valuable skills that one day can be used to start your own business.

After shouting out your request, take a minute or two to envision your request as if it were already occurring in your life. Immerse yourself in the details of your desires and preferences. Your belief in your vision will greatly enhance this process.

In response to your request, the universe has granted it. A giant hand reaches out of the sky to offer you a gift box. Accept the gift box and place it in a basket.

If you have more than one request, repeat the process of asking your divine helper for guidance, silently shouting out your request into the blue sky, envisioning it as if it's already true and receiving a gift box.

When you are done, thank your divine helper for their guidance and participation. Stand up and bring the basket filled with gift boxes with you as you descend the grassy hill, heading back towards the tunnel entrance. Turn away from the tunnel, and then walk through the white mist to return to this reality.

I recommend you do this exercise every day for 10-15 minutes (or longer if you're enjoying yourself). You don't always have to ask for something when you do this exercise — sometimes sitting with your divine helper while enjoying the view can be beneficial for your soul.

You can ask your divine helper for guidance on...

- **Life Direction:** Seek guidance on major life decisions such as career choices, educational pursuits or relocation.

- **Relationships:** Ask for insight and clarity regarding personal relationships, including friendships, romantic partnerships and family dynamics.

- **Health and Wellness:** Request guidance on matters related to physical, mental and emotional well-being, including health concerns and lifestyle choices.

- **Spiritual Growth:** Seek guidance on deepening your spiritual practice, connecting with your higher self or exploring existential questions.

- **Financial Matters:** Ask for guidance on financial decisions, budgeting, investments or career advancement opportunities.

- **Creative Pursuits:** Request inspiration and direction for creative projects, artistic endeavors or entrepreneurial ventures.

- **Personal Development:** Seek guidance on areas of personal growth and self-improvement, such as overcoming challenges, building confidence or developing new skills.

- **Conflict Resolution:** Ask for assistance in navigating conflicts or resolving disputes in a peaceful and harmonious manner.

- **Life Challenges:** Request guidance on how to cope with difficult situations, setbacks or obstacles you may be facing.

- **Gratitude and Blessings:** Express gratitude for blessings in your life and ask for guidance on how to cultivate a mindset of gratitude and abundance.

- **Whatever else is on your mind.**

Connecting with God

"What you seek is seeking you." Rumi

One summer afternoon, while my parents were getting ready to run errands and my younger brother was wandering into the kitchen, my 14-year-old self was lying on the living room carpet wondering if there was a limit to how small a physical particle could be. Did matter get smaller forever?

To see for myself, I envisioned going inside my body, viewing its inner workings. I saw multiple types of cells with blood cells moving quickly past them. I focused on a single blood cell, which was bright-red, filled with oxygen-rich hemoglobin. I examined its membrane, zooming inside to its inner workings. I kept zooming in on each particle, going deeper into the world of atoms. Then, unexpectedly, I reached the end of physical matter and saw a golden light that I knew was God's essence. This light did not have a face, yet I knew it was looking at me, pleased I had discovered it. I only viewed this sight for a moment before I snapped out of it.

I was awed that a simple curiosity led to such a profound connection with God.

This experience showed me that we can connect with God if we go deep within ourselves to where the barriers of the physical world can be transcended.

> "Deep within you is everything that is perfect, ready to radiate through you and out into the world." W-pI.41.3.1

> "Let them all go, dancing in the wind, dipping and turning till they disappear from sight, far, far outside of you. And turn you to the stately calm within, where in holy stillness dwells the living God you never left, and Who never left you. The Holy Spirit takes you gently by the hand, and retraces with you your mad journey outside yourself, leading you gently back to the truth and safety within." T-18.I.8.1-3

The next two exercises will help you connect with God.

Exercise — Connecting with God

"All that you seek is already within you. In Hinduism it is called the Atman, in Buddhism the pure Buddha-Mind. Christ said, 'the kingdom of heaven is within you.' Quakers call it the 'still small voice within.' This is the space of full awareness that is in harmony with all the universe, and thus is wisdom itself." Ram Dass

This personal journey will transcend all worldly concerns and guide you to connect with God. It's crucial to dedicate time to this, as all the riches in the world hold no value without His loving embrace.

To begin this exercise, sit quietly with your eyes closed for three to five minutes. At the beginning of the practice period, repeat very slowly, **"God goes with me wherever I go."** Then, make no effort to think of anything. Try, instead, to get a sense of turning inward, past all the idle thoughts of the world. Try to enter very deeply into your own mind, keeping it clear of any thoughts that might divert your attention.

From time to time, you may repeat "God goes with me wherever I go," if you find it helpful. But most of all, try to sink down and inward, away from the world and all the foolish thoughts of the world. You are trying to reach past all these things. You are trying to leave appearances and approach reality.

It is quite possible to reach God. In fact it is very easy, because it is the most natural thing in the world. You might even say it is the only natural thing in the world. The way will open, if you believe it is possible. This exercise can bring very startling results even the first time it is attempted, and sooner or later it is always successful. It will never fail completely and instant success is possible.

This exercise is paraphrased from ACIM's Workbook Lesson 41.

Exercise — Bringing in the Divine Power

Contrasting with the previous exercise, which focused on introspection to connect with God, this exercise invites you to draw the divine power into yourself — an approach that can deepen your spiritual connection.

To begin this exercise, take slow deep breaths with your eyes closed. Point your eyes upwards toward heaven while keeping your eyelids closed.

Say a prayer to Jesus and ask Him to bring heaven down to you.

Watch your breath as you inhale and exhale. Remember to keep your eyes pointed upwards. If you notice that your eyes have lowered, point them upwards again. This will raise your consciousness to the top of your head or just above it.

Continue watching your breath.

Stay in the present moment. If your mind drifts, simply begin watching your breath again and double-check that your eyes are pointed upwards.

The aim of this exercise is to establish a connection with the divine power. When this connection is made, the experiences can vary greatly. Some may feel a pressure at the top of their head, which then spreads throughout their body. Others might experience a sense of profound joy or ecstasy. It's important to note that the timing of this connection is unique to each individual. It could happen on your first attempt or it might take several weeks or even months. Remember, everyone's journey is different.

Regardless of the sensations or emotional impact, once you connect to the divine power, it will be easier to connect the next time you do this exercise.

Summary of the Miraculous Life Process

"The mind is everything. What you think,

you become." Buddha

Miracles are your divine right. When you understand the fundamentals of manifesting and do it with the help of the Holy Spirit, Jesus and divine helpers, you become a miracle worker who creates a life for yourself that is filled with happiness, well-being and abundance.

Highlights of the Miraculous Life Process:

- Your thoughts have the power to alter your life. When combined with strong belief, they become extremely powerful.

- The Holy Spirit, Jesus and divine helpers will work alongside you to manifest your heartfelt desires.

This means you don't have to make decisions alone, because they are more than willing to guide you. Their advice will save you time so you can focus on what's important.

- Your thoughts are more powerful than your actions.

- You need to be mindful of the random thoughts running through your mind.

- Positive thoughts are in harmony with your higher self, negative thoughts are not.

- There is enough abundance for everyone. You don't have to worry about taking too much for yourself when you are co-creating with the Holy Spirit, because when you win, everyone wins.

- You can use emotions as a barometer to guide your decisions.

- You need to ask for what you want.

- You should act when inspired.

- Your actions should feel pleasing to you.

- Releasing blockages improves manifestation results by removing the barriers between you and the Creative powers, allowing abundance to flow freely.

- The time delay prevents what you are thinking about from manifesting instantaneously. This allows you time to re-evaluate your thoughts and make changes if they aren't harmonious with your higher self.

- You must envision your desires as if they are true now. Otherwise, you project them into the distant future — always out of reach.

- Set clear goals.

- Don't let fear stop you from following your heart.

- To manifest your desires successfully, focus on what you want *daily*.

Basic Steps of the Miraculous Life Process

Positive thoughts and emotions create desirable results. Negative thoughts and emotions create undesirable results. Thinking about what you don't want is the same as asking for it so only think about what you want.

You need to forgive your past because your lingering negative thoughts and emotions act as blockages between you and the Creative powers. To heal your past with the Holy Spirit's help, use the exercise "Releasing the Blockages."

The Holy Spirit, Jesus and divine helpers are always available to guide you through your decisions. You simply need to ask them for help, which will save you valuable time and avoid undesirable experiences.

To get inspired with new ideas, try the "Discovering What You Want" exercise. Take notes of any inspiration you receive, and then create a list of the most important points. Review the list every day until you figure out what you want to do.

Once you know what you want to achieve, visualize your desires as if they were already true on a daily basis.

Alternatively, you can perform the "The Secret to Miraculous Results" exercise, which will help accelerate you towards success with the assistance of your divine helper.

Finally, when you feel inspired, take action!

Mistakes Will be Made and That's Okay

Changing your state of mind doesn't happen overnight. You'll forget to manifest when you're busy or simply because it's not a habit yet. Don't beat yourself up, just get back on track.

We've all had days when we bumped our heads getting out of bed, and then the day kept getting worse. It's our response that prevents a rocky start from spiraling out of control. Ideally, after bumping your head (and taking a moment to soothe your bump), you would remind yourself that things can go smoothly and the minor setback will not set the tone for the rest of the day.

Take a moment to pray for guidance, and then envision your perfect day. My favorite way to start the day is to say this prayer, "Please guide my day. Help me to know where to go, what to do and what to say."

When you don't take the time to "reset" after something bad happens, it becomes a self-fulfilling prophecy of having a bad day. The hardest part of the Miraculous Life Process will be reacting with an empowered state of mind while something negative is happening, but this is how undesirable circumstances are transformed into something miraculous.

Earlier in this book, I told the story of my mother's passing and how her pension had been given to my sister. I was extremely upset, but my first response was to pray to the Holy Spirit to take away my anger. Through relentless repetition of prayer, I experienced the most remarkable miracle of my life — the Holy Instant. The overwhelming presence of love dissolved my anger.

I needed to ask for help because there was no way I was going to release that intense anger on my own. Relying on the Holy Spirit allowed me to stay in a state of grace and prevented me from doing or saying something I would have regretted. The situation would have gotten a lot worse if I hadn't taken the time to pray for help and healing immediately.

The Course says the ego speaks first, and then the Holy Spirit responds by offering the alternative of a better dream. Keep in mind that the Dream is rolling along, offering us events based on its fear-based foundation. It's up to us to remember we are the dreamers and not a captive of the original Dream. We can always choose another, better alternative. So don't let a negative event dissuade you from manifesting it into something positive. The ego wants you to feel powerless because it wants to extend the original Dream as long as possible. Once the Dream ends, the ego ends.

The ego doesn't know about the Holy Spirit or how He is working with you to offer you better versions of the Dream. The ego only knows when your attention is not focused on it. Once it senses you are not listening to it, the ego will try to get your attention by inflaming your thoughts with unloving ones. You have to decide which voice you will listen to, the ego's or the Holy Spirit's. When a negative situation or thought presents itself, respond by asking the Holy Spirit for guidance, strength and healing, and stay focused on the positive aspects of your life and desires. Don't let the ego distract you. Your consistent and heartfelt dedication will create miraculous shifts in your life.

In Conclusion

What I learned the most from the Miraculous Life Process is that when we deliberately keep certain aspects of our lives separate from the Holy Spirit, we are actually holding back parts of ourselves under the pretense that they are not "spiritual" and, therefore, it's okay to keep them to ourselves. This way of thinking is a product of the ego. Instead, if we allow every aspect of our lives to be guided by the Holy Spirit, Jesus and divine helpers, we can experience and realize things that we wouldn't have been able to otherwise. This will enable us to align ourselves with love instead of fear, and open our mind to the abundance of goodness the divine power offers.

When we manifest with the Divine, we can awaken from the Dream much sooner. According to the Course, we could save millions of years, which oddly makes me concerned about how long we'll be trapped in this Dream, but I digress because you and I could wake up in an instant.

While writing this book, I tried to keep in mind that all our achievements will turn to dust, and the only thing that is real in this world is love. However, we still have to pay our bills, interact with friends and family and recycle our milk cartons, so let's make the best of it and manifest a life filled with happiness, well-being, abundance and, most importantly, love.

I challenge you to follow the principles and exercises outlined in this book every day for the next 60 days. The 60-day journal in the following chapter will assist you in reflecting, staying on track and forming good habits. After experiencing the positive outcomes, I hope you will be motivated to continue the Miraculous Life Process for the remainder of your life.

Journal — 60-Days of Reflection

The main objective of keeping a journal is to tap into your inner wisdom and allow your thoughts and insights to flow naturally. Writing in your journal every day will strengthen your ability to manifest your goals.

Day 1   What am I grateful for in my life right now?

____

____

____

____

Day 2   Reflect on the analogy of life as a movie with alternate scenes. How does this analogy deepen my understanding of choice and potentiality within the world?

____

____

____

____

Day 3   What limiting beliefs are holding me back from manifesting my desires? How can I release my limiting beliefs and replace them with empowering ones?

____

____

____

____

____

Day 4   Contemplate the core concepts of the Miraculous Life Process, particularly the power of the mind to create and the importance of aligning thoughts with love and truth. How do these concepts resonate with my experiences and beliefs?

____

____

____

____

Day 5   What does abundance mean to me?

____

____

____

____

____

Day 6   How can I change my thoughts, words and actions to improve my efforts to attract abundance?

____

____

____

____

____

Day 7   What are my core beliefs about manifesting, and how do they influence my manifestation efforts?

____

____

____

____

____

Day 8   What fears do I need to overcome to manifest my desires fully?

____

____

____

____

____

Day 9   How do I determine if my thoughts are loving or unloving?

____

____

____

____

____

Day 10 Reflect on the role of forgiveness and healing to remove my blockages, allowing abundance, joy and health to flow freely into my life. How can the practice of forgiveness contribute to my spiritual growth?

____

____

____

____

Day 11 What does success look and feel like to me?

____

____

____

____

____

Day 12 How can I maintain my positive thoughts to attract positive experiences into my life?

____

____

____

____

____

Day 13 What spiritual practice(s) can I use to nourish my soul?

____

____

____

____

____

Day 14   How can I cultivate a belief that I am worthy and deserving?

____

____

____

____

____

Day 15   What blessings have I received recently that I may have overlooked?

____

____

____

____

____

Day 16   List three things I could do today that would move me closer toward manifesting my goals.

____

____

____

____

____

____

Day 17   To make maximum progress in the manifestation process, I will repeat the exercise "Releasing the Blockages" (in this book). Below is what I was able to release.

____

____

____

____

Day 18   Reflect on the concept of miracles as my divine right. How does this perspective empower me to embrace my inherent ability to manifest a miraculous life?

Day 19   What role does belief play in the manifestation process?

Day 20   Write down three negative emotions/situations from my week on a scrap piece of paper. Tear or burn the paper to release them from my mind. How do I feel afterward?

____

____

____

____

Day 21   Consider the idea that manifesting my life is not only possible, but something I am already doing. How does this realization influence my approach to intentional manifestation and co-creation with the Holy Spirit?

____

____

____

____

Day 22   How do I define happiness, and how can I invite more of it into my life?

____

____

____

____

____

____

Day 23   What aspects of life do I believe can be changed in my destiny? Why?

____

____

____

____

____

Day 24   How can I let go of control and surrender to God's Will?

____

____

____

____

____

Day 25   What recent signs and synchronicities have I noticed that affirm my manifestations are becoming a reality?

____

____

____

____

____

Day 26   How have my visualization efforts enhanced my manifestation practice?

____

____

____

____

____

____

Day 27   Reflect on the idea that every thought contains power, particularly when it is combined with strong emotions and beliefs. How does this awareness influence my practice of mindfulness and intentional manifestation?

____

____

____

____

Day 28   List the abundance in my life, including relationships, health and finances, and then say a prayer of gratitude for all that I have.

____

____

____

____

____

Day 29   What do I need to release to make space for new blessings to enter my life?

____

____

____

____

____

Day 30   Write "I am grateful for my abundance" six times while feeling gratitude in my heart.

____

____

____

____

____

____

Day 31   What are my heart's deepest desires?

____

____

____

____

____

Day 32 How can I transmute fear into faith and trust?

____

____

____

____

____

Day 33 What are the blessings in disguise I might be overlooking?

____

____

____

____

____

Day 34   How do I distinguish between thoughts influenced by my ego and those guided by the Holy Spirit in my daily decision-making process?

____

____

____

____

____

Day 35   What do I need to forgive myself for in order to move forward?

____

____

____

____

____

Day 36   Explore the importance of visualizing my heart's desires as if they were already true now. How does this daily practice influence the manifestation process and the outcomes I attract into my life?

____

____

____

____

Day 37   What small acts of kindness can I perform today?

____

____

____

____

____

____

Day 38   What doubts do I have about the Miraculous Life Process? Why? How can I overcome them?

____

____

____

____

____

Day 39   What patterns or habits no longer serve my highest good and how can I release them?

____

____

____

____

____

Day 40   How can I strengthen my intuition and trust its guidance in the manifestation process?

173

____

____

____

____

____

Day 41   What role does surrender play in allowing manifestations to unfold?

____

____

____

____

____

Day 42   How can I remain open to unexpected opportunities and blessings?

____

____

____

____

____

Day 43   What messages are the Holy Spirit, Jesus and divine helpers trying to communicate to me through my heart?

____

____

____

____

____

Day 44   Explore the concept of time as a safety valve in the manifestation process. How does this understanding alleviate my fears and uncertainties about the possibility of my thoughts manifesting immediately?

____

____

____

____

Day 45   What are the qualities I admire in others that I can cultivate within myself?

____

____

____

____

____

Day 46   How can I create a sacred space for meditating, visualizing or praying?

____

____

____

____

____

____

Day 47   What fears arise when I consider fully stepping into my power, and how can I overcome them?

____

____

____

____

____

Day 48   How can I use my gifts and talents to serve others and contribute to the greater good?

177

Day 49   What does it mean to live in alignment with God's Will?

Day 50   How can I surrender the need for validation from others and instead trust in my own worthiness?

____

____

____

____

____

Day 51   What steps can I take to release my attachment to specific outcomes and trust in God's plan for me?

____

____

____

____

____

Day 52   Reflect on the idea that the Holy Spirit can alter time. How does this perspective offer hope and encouragement?

____

____

____

____

____

____

Day 53   What past successes can I draw upon as evidence of my ability to manifest my desires?

____

____

____

____

____

Day 54   Contemplate the ways in which the Divine communicates with me. How can I cultivate stillness and receptivity to better hear divine guidance?

____

____

____

____

Day 55   What role does self-love play in the manifestation process and how can I cultivate it more fully?

____

____

____

____

____

Day 56   How can I overcome procrastination and take consistent action towards my goals?

____

____

____

____

____

Day 57   What emotions do I need to process so that I can release my resistance and invite in abundance?

____

____

____

____

____

Day 58 Reflect on the idea that when I gain, everyone gains. How does this perspective shift my understanding of abundance and interconnectedness with others?

____

____

____

____

____

Day 59 Reflecting on the importance of taking action in the Miraculous Life Process, how can I align my actions with divine guidance and opportunities to manifest my desires?

____

____

____

____

Day 60   What changes have occurred in my life since
I began the Miraculous Life Process?

183

____

____

____

____

____

____

From this point forward, start your own journal to document your journey to a miraculous life!

Explanation of the ACIM Annotation System

Many of the verses that appear in this book were taken from *A Course in Miracles* (ACIM). Including them was meant to provide additional insights and justify the author's claims. You may have your own interpretations because the Holy Spirit leads everyone in their own way. The following examples illustrate the ACIM annotation system.

Here is an example of a verse from the Workbook section:

"It is impossible that anything should come to me unbidden by myself. Even in this world, it is I who rule my destiny. What happens is what I desire." W-pII.253.1.1-3

- W = Workbook
- pII = part II of the Workbook
- 253 = Lesson 253
- 1 = Paragraph 1
- 1-3 = Lines 1-3 (each sentence is a line)

Here is an example from the Text:

"The Holy Spirit asks of you but this; bring to Him every secret you have locked away from Him. Open every door to Him, and bid Him enter the darkness and lighten it away." T-14.VII.6.1-2

- T = Text
- 14 = Chapter 14
- VII = Section VII
- 6 = Paragraph 6
- 1-2 = Lines 1-2

Here is an example from the Manual for Teachers:

"Those who are certain of the outcome can afford to wait, and wait without anxiety." M-4.VIII.1.1

- M = Manual for Teachers
- 4 = Question 4
- VIII = Section VIII
- 1 = Paragraph 1
- 1 = Line 1

Additional abbreviations:

- r = Review (workbook)
- fl = Final Lessons (workbook)
- C = Clarification of Terms (in the Manual for Teachers)
- ep = Epilogues (end of Workbook and Clarification of Terms

Overview of Shamanism and Shamanic Journeying

Shamanism is the oldest known spiritual practice and is still practiced today by indigenous people on every continent. While there are many different rituals, one commonality is that the shaman acts as a catalyst between this world and the spirit world. Ultimately, both are an illusion, but while we are trapped within this Dream, divine helpers are needed to help us not only wake up, but heal.

In the book, *Awakening to the Spirit World*, Sandra Ingerman and Hank Wesselman offered this insight: "Shamanism is an ancient and powerful spiritual practice that can help us thrive during challenging and changing times. In our modern-day technological world we have been led to believe that what we see, touch, hear, smell, and taste with our ordinary senses connects us only to the world that is visible around us. Conversely, shamanism teaches that there are doorways into other realms of reality where helping spirits reside who can share guidance, insight, and healing not just for ourselves but also for the world in which we live."

Shamanism is a profound spiritual practice in which shamans utilize visionary processes to traverse the spirit realm. Within this realm, they engage with a diverse array of entities, including spirit guides, ancestors and enlightened beings.

Power animals serve as steadfast companions and guardians, lending their archetype power to the shaman's quests. The spirit realm's triadic division into lower, middle and upper worlds offers varied experiences, each valuable in its own right and suited to different needs and intentions. Through these shamanic journeys, shamans navigate the intricate web of existence, facilitating healing, wisdom and connection with the Divine.

My personal journey with shamanism has been life-changing. The connection to divine energy has opened my mind to the wonders of the unseen world, which affects every aspect of our lives and even the entire universe. Through shamanism, I have come to understand the interconnectedness of all beings — the earth, sky, nature, animals, winged and sea creatures and mankind — singing one song of unending love.

About the Author

Elizabeth M. Herrera is a shamanic healer and teacher, and author of *Shaman Stone Soup* (memoir), *Dreams of Heaven* (Spiritual Fantasy), *Earth Sentinels: The Storm Creators* (Fantasy), and *Of Stars and Clay* (Fantasy).

She grew up in a Christian home, but lost her faith in her early twenties. For over a decade, she searched for something to fill the void, eventually discovering Native American spirituality (shamanism). Through this spiritual practice, she unexpectedly became a catalyst for healing and miracles. These experiences led her back to a belief in God.

Elizabeth began her shamanic path in 2002. She continued her studies through the Foundation for Shamanic Studies for shamanic journeying, soul retrieval, and death and dying (psychopomp), but her major source of learning has been from her spirit guides, who offer limitless guidance and lessons on living a more spiritual life. She is also a student of *A Course in Miracles*, which she discovered is the perfect companion for shamanism.